interruption |the brief|

The LA+ INTERRUPTION international design ideas competition invited designers to take an established place and design something that productively interrupts both its cultural and spatial context to challenge the status quo and redirect ecological or socio-economic flows.

Results within

4   EDITORIAL
    RICHARD WELLER + TATUM L. HANDS

6   LET'S SMOKE, WALK, AND ENTER COMPETITIONS
    KATYA CRAWFORD

12 THE JURY: UNINTERRUPTED
    FIONA RABY, MARTIN REIN-CANO, RANIA GHOSN,
    MARK RAGGATT + JASON ZHISEN HO

22 WINNING ENTRIES

24 FIRST PRIZE
    XIANGYU LIU, CHENGXI ZHA + CHENGYUAN XU

30 SECOND PRIZE
    JAKE BOSWELL

36 THIRD PRIZE
    ANTOINE APRUZZESE, THOMAS ROCHE + ANNE KLEPAL

40 HONORABLE MENTIONS

42 JOSEPH HENRY KENNEDY JR., VINCENT PARLATORE +
    HANA SVATOŠ-RAŽNJEVIC

46 QIUTONG HUANG + JINGJUN TAO

50 JONATHAN ARNABOLDI

54 OLIVIA PINNER + ADAM SCOTT

58 LILLIAN CHUNG KWAN YU, WONG OI LING ELLENA
    + ZICHENG KAI ZHAO

62 JIAQI LI + LEYI CUI

66 XIAOJUN ZHANG + PETER W. FERRETTO

70 EUGENE ONG

74 YANG DU + SCOTT AKER

78 ALLEGRA ZANIRATO + REBECCA BILLI

82 SALON DES REFUSES

    UPCOMING ISSUES

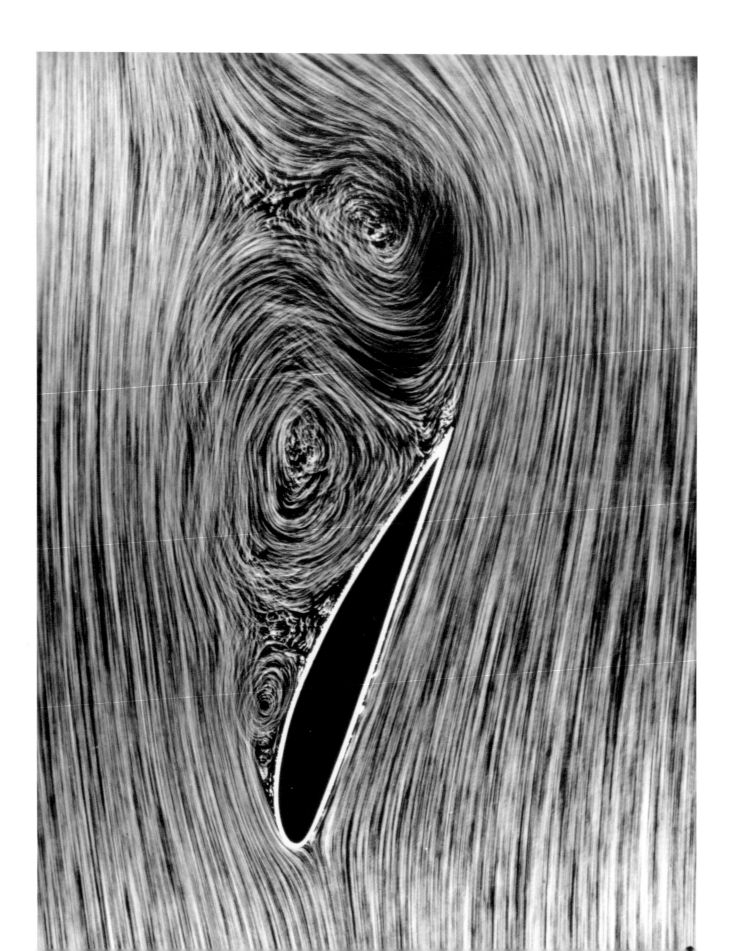

LA+ INTERRUPTION
EDITORIAL

LA+ INTERRUPTION is the fourth international design competition we've conducted. We believe there is great value in these competitions. They offer designers opportunities to develop their own ideas and methods, and then see their work in the context of their peers. In the feature essay for this issue, Katya Crawford–who, together with Kathleen Kambic, is currently writing a book on the subject–champions ideas competitions as a vital element of contemporary design culture. For her, they are less about "winning" and more about self-development, and despite–or perhaps because of–the physical and mental pain of producing a viable competition entry, she argues they are exalted and ultimately pleasurable experiences. We agree.

Unlike most competitions, LA+ makes a point of publishing the results of its competitions and interviewing the jury to get their feedback. For example, in her response Fiona Raby of the Parsons School of Design In New York says that for her the most important and appealing submissions were those that sought empathy with the nonhuman. Mark Raggatt of ARM Architecture in Australia asks, "What would a city of empathy really look like?" Raggatt then turns the table on the design professions by calling for interruptions to their complacency. Rania Ghosn of Design Earth and MIT, underscores the act of design as a material and political interruption of the status quo. Martin Rein Cano of TOPOTEK 1 in Berlin explains that in his own practice he seeks to enhance the latent energy of places, noting that this often emerges from working with, instead of against, conflict. Finally, Jason Ho of SCUT in Guangzhou, reminds us that bigger is certainly not always better. For Ho, the most incisive interruptions are often the smallest, and as such he urges designers to aim for greater intimacy and precision in their work.

Ho's point is well taken, and it must be said there isn't a lot of precision in the majority of entries in this competition. And yes, we can and should be critical of this work for this is another useful function of these competitions. In entering a competition you put your work up for peer review. Even though competitions such as this do allow for and encourage speculation and provocation, an ideas competition is not a license for incomprehensible vagary, or superficiality. Entering an ideas competition means developing and taking responsibility for ideas. Unlike professional practice, the ideas competition calls upon entrants to spend maximum time with design ideation and less on technical resolution. That said, ideas also need to be "resolved" and, unless the brief demands otherwise, juries also expect ideas to be grounded in at least a basic awareness of feasibility.

The three winning designs each balance the tension between idea and reality, but with very different degrees of emphasis across the spectrum between the two. Xiangyu Liu, Chengxi Zha, and Cengyuan Xu's winning design–a proposal for a massive carbon sequestration curtain bisecting Manhattan–has clearly benefited most from the lack of practicality that an ideas competition affords. In second place, Jake Boswell's proposal to tap the latent energy of dams using a mix of available technologies strikes a more even balance. The third-place entry by Antoine Apruzzese, Thomas Roche, and Anne Klepal is almost banal in its buildability, yet what it lacks in terms of formal and technical experimentation it makes up for with plausible political potential.

In addition to identifying winners, it is important to have a sizeable batch of honorable mentions. These are entries that some, but not all judges, considered, for one reason or another, to be outstanding. A straight-up list of these shows the range and richness of the entries this competition attracted: a city-scale "play carpet," an algorithm for DIY renovations, rewilding in Milan, a Christo-like covering for oil refineries, a dystopia of "mole people" mining water under Vegas, a postindustrial nursery in China, a memorial to the lost agricultural way of life in China, the relocation of the Lebanese parliament into ruins, a reworking of the geometry of slave plantations, and finally, a happy twist on sea level rise in Lisbon. On the one hand this range is exciting, on the other it made for difficult judging and as we reflect on the results it is possible to conclude that our brief was too open-ended.

Finally, there is the marvelous kaleidoscope of the Salon des Refusés – literally, the exhibition of rejects. In this section we gather submissions that were of real interest to one or more judges but were ultimately rejected by the jury. Be that as it may, in the Salon we find a beautiful array of seeds that one day might grow a wilder, more exotic garden.

LA+ congratulates not only the authors of all the published projects but all entrants. Everyone who took the trouble to enter such a competition deserves to be acknowledged because in being as open-ended as it was, this was not an easy brief. And if there is just one thing that we hope that all entrants got out of this exercise it is a small taste of inventing your own projects, a taste of interrupting the status quo, where we otherwise wait passively for someone else to tell us what to do. LA+ also thanks the jury – a truly interesting line up of practitioners and academics whose work has proven the value of being brave enough to interrupt.

Tatum L. Hands + Richard Weller
Issue Editors

KATYA CRAWFORD

LET'S SMOKE, WALK, AND
ENTER COMPETITIONS

Katya Crawford is professor and chair of the Department of Landscape Architecture at the University of New Mexico and past-president and fellow of The Council of Educators in Landscape Architecture. She has lectured and exhibited her work nationally and internationally and is currently coauthoring a book titled *The Design Competition in Landscape Architecture: A Guide for Schools and Firms* (2023).

+ LANDSCAPE ARCHITECTURE, DESIGN

Poet Billy Collins declared the best cigarette as the one when he had a "little something going on in the typewriter," an idea forming, a poem blooming. He fills his coffee cup, lights his cigarette...

> That was the best cigarette,
> when I would steam into the study
> full of vaporous hope
> and stand there,
> the big headlamp of my face
> pointed down at all the words in parallel lines.[1]

What does smoking have to do with design competitions? For many, nothing – at least not now in the 21st century, knowing what we do. What we can all relate to is the spark, the joy, the rush of a concept blooming on paper. We work with it in its infancy, push it to grow, knead it, give it structure, manipulate it, question it, start to tell its story, let it rest, and go back to it. Competitions *interrupt* the status quo by giving designers the opportunity to stretch boundaries, to test new ideas, to form new partnerships, to speculate.

In a recent interview, Walter Hood expressed the value of speculation–the "what if?"–and how speculation is sluggish within the practice and education of landscape architecture.[2] The design of physical places is being approached as a problem to be solved, with words such as resiliency, global warming, and social justice propping up the solution. While no one can argue that those words are connected to the most pressing issues of our time, saying them won't guarantee change and repeatedly saying them might actually dilute their importance.

Ideas competitions can offer an open door to speculation, theory, debate, and joy. LA+ competitions invite us to walk through this door. The competition LA+ IMAGINATION (2017) called for the design of an island no larger than one square kilometer. The wildly popular second competition, LA+ ICONOCLAST (2018), boldly set forth a challenge to redesign New York's beloved Central Park after eco-terrorists had obliterated the iconic landscape. LA+ CREATURE (2020) charged entrants with designing for nonhuman clients. LA+ INTERRUPTION (2022)–the latest LA+ competition and the subject of this issue–called for an interruption of any scale within any city or place that disrupts its spatial and cultural contexts. Do you get excited by reading the titles and pithy charges of these ideas competitions? I certainly do.

While the submission requirements are minimal, the competition briefs demand rigorous research, a theoretical stance, imagination, and visual and written clarity. The challenge to speculate via design is a necessary defibrillator to the core of a design education and to the profession. But instead of resetting a failing heart, speculation has the potential to reset the global dominance of a capitalist agenda from endless production, consumption, and destruction.

The role of imagery backed by research and a clearly communicated theoretical stance is integral to the competition, and to the messy, expanding definition of landscape architecture and its agency in the world. Image-making is largely what competitions call for. Image creation also dominates what landscape architects do, and each type of image plays a distinct role in the theory and making of landscape. James Corner wrote about this in his still-relevant essay "Projection and Disclosure in Drawing," published in *Landscape Architecture Magazine* in 1993.[3] There, he discusses the problems inherent in treating drawing as a noun instead of a verb – the drawing is a "thing" that is a technical drawing on one end of the spectrum and a fine art object on the other end. The potential of a drawing as a verb to critically engage in an activity of "seeing or projecting" is much more powerful. Creating an image that explores, explains, projects, and invites the viewer into the story is foundational in working through a competition. The drawing set must capture the competition jury's attention and must prompt them to see the world anew...at least if you are to have a chance at winning. But winning is not the primary value in entering competitions. The process of discovery for the makers, and the sharing of ideas in an active manner is where the magic lies. Think of it as taking a daily walk to lose weight. If that is the goal, you may speed up the gait and walk for a longer distance. But to go for a walk *for the sake of walking* can inspire a deeper connection to the environment in which one lives. You may begin to notice what has become invisible in your busy life. You slow down and observe the change in seasonal light, the temperature, the surface beneath your feet, the neighborhood soundtrack as it shifts with the seasons, the domesticated and wild creatures you live among, new plants, and old neighbors.

But back to the image, a primary element of the design competition. Both the production image and the built landscape can have a dark side: gentrification, the conscious or unconscious perpetuation of oppressive cultural narratives, the superficial objectification of people and places. Typically, we see images depicting a perpetual, daytime summer with the same people lifted off Google in various passive and active poses. Academia and the profession are both guilty here. Perspectives or vignettes are now called "renders" with the inevitable technological advances of rendering software. "Rendering" could have been the digital replacement for the term "drawing," but the term didn't stand a chance. Instead, "render" reigns, shifting the verb into the noun – the object. In this predicament of rendering or renders, one must be careful not to let technology transform the creative process of making into a perfunctory act of producing a visually consumable, hyper-realistic object. Visual representation can be a game of trickery, or it can be a challenging, poetic invitation – an authentic inquiry. Images are powerful–powerfully good or powerfully bad–and never benign. The beauty of this power, for environmental designers, activists, and artists is that the image does indeed have the ability to represent, from multiple perspectives, the world in which we want to live.

Both students and professionals enter the LA+ competitions. For students, they are either taking on the challenge at hand as part of a class or on their own, in addition to their coursework. Either way, the hundreds of entries denote a thirst for speculative projects. In UNM's Department of Landscape Architecture, where I write from, competitions are built into the studio sequence. We have evaluated their importance as a teaching and learning armature through the work process and product, as well as through conversing with students about their experiences. The benefits are numerous. The students love the opportunity to take on projects that leap over local boundaries, to pour over briefs written by outside designers, engage with a global design community, explore their creative process, and strengthen their writing skills. They love winning too.

While competition directly implies pitting one person/designer against another, the opposite of competition–*collaboration*–is the unsung hero of the competition story. Rarely is a competition entry produced and won by a sole author, and even when it is, it is likely the individual received critical feedback and prompts from a peer or instructor. Both seasoned and novice designers intentionally or unintentionally rub together causing friction and support, igniting debate, furthering the conversation, and improving their knowledge, ideation, and proposition. In an educational setting, collaboration–in tandem with developing graphic, written, and intellectual skills–helps prepare the student for practice outside the walls of academia.

For professionals, one would have to assume that the reason to enter an LA+ competition is for stimulation and joy as there is no chance that a paying contract will come out of a winning entry. Joy, simple joy (as described by Billy Collins), and complex joy–comfort with discomfort, learning something new, realizing difficult truths, shaking the ground we thought was solid, seeing possibilities with new eyes, and exhaustion and energy from making–is the real gift of design speculation for students, educators, and professionals alike. As an example, I would not have given much thought to or felt any empathy toward locusts had it not been for one student's exquisite, short animation of a locust asking for human understanding as part of his process work for the LA+ CREATURE competition.[4] This student connected our small, 2020 online cohort to deep time, revealing the role that the now extinct Rocky Mountain locust played in transforming the prehistoric seabed of the Great Plains into the planet's most fertile topsoil, while simultaneously discussing the irony of industrialized agriculture being one of the biggest culprits to the climate crisis, creating perfect conditions for locust swarms in less industrialized countries. Engaging in the LA+ CREATURE competition was at once an antidote to the pandemic condition and a mirror back to us.

But let's back up. Ideas competitions are only one type of competition among many. There are open call competitions that present a proposition for designers of all fields to tackle.

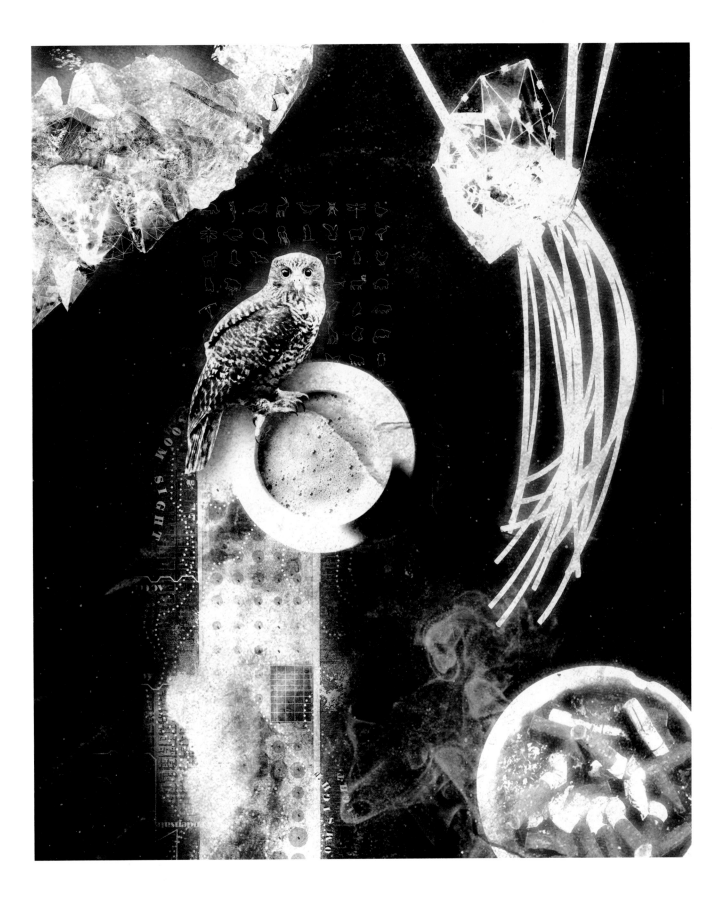

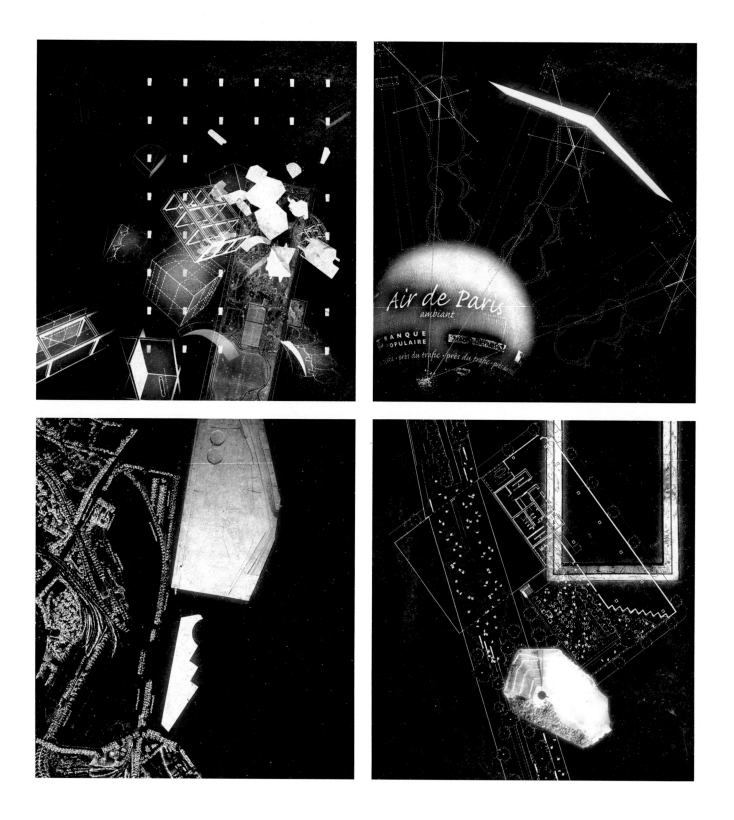

An organizing body puts forth the competition with the hopes of harnessing a wide range of ideas. The competition can end after prizes are given out and winning entries published, or it can move into a second phase of invited participants. New York City's High Line (2004) is one such example. Another scenario is the competition winner receiving a contract and the project getting built – such as Bernard Tschumi's Parc de la Villette (1982). A third type of competition is by invitation, where a deliberate selection of designers is asked to compete by the client's advising firm. In this scenario, funding is provided to each firm to cover the costs invested in developing a proposition. The funding rarely covers the complete costs, but it is certainly less risky than pouring time, labor, and materials into a project that you may not get a contract for. A fourth type, popular in Europe, works similarly to an RFQ (request for qualifications) in the United States. The request is called a "competition" and is run through multiple competitive stages until the winner is chosen for the contract. In a recent interview with Agence Ter's Henri Bava, he stated that their Paris-based firm enters approximately 60 competitions a year.[5]

While I have stressed the value of simply entering competitions, it would be wrong to ignore the euphoria and life-changing course winning can have on an individual or firm. My own small wins with friends and colleagues have resulted in leaping and whooping into the air upon finding out, ecstatic hugs, squealing phone calls, and rushes of validation. And I have no doubt that the wins played a large role in my case for tenure. For young firms, winning can launch practitioners into stardom. Take Maya Lin, just 21 and still an undergraduate student at Yale University when she won the Vietnam Veteran's Memorial competition. Snøhetta's Craig Dykers, Christoph Kapeller, and Kjetil Thorsen winning the Alexandria Library Competition (1989) without a doubt set the foundation for their multi-disciplinary practice to soar in the design world. Winning competitions helped Kate Orff start her practice, SCAPE. In her words, it was "a great confidence booster" as she started her practice with a rented desk and a sign on the door.[6] As Richard Weller wrote in his short piece "Winning and Losing" in *250 Things a Landscape Architect Should Know*, "One of the great highs in a career is winning your first design competition. In a sea of doubt it is a moment of pure, intoxicating validation coming directly from a panel of eminent and most excellent judges."[7]

There is no question that some of the most remarkable, paradigm-changing designed landscapes came into existence through the competition process: Manhattan's Central Park (Fredrick Law Olmsted and Calvert Vaux, 1857), Paris's Parc de la Villette (Bernard Tschumi, 1982) and Parc André Citroën (Alain Provost and Gilles Clement, 1985), Washington DC's Vietnam Veterans Memorial (Maya Lin, 1982), Duisburg-Nord's Landshaftspark (Latz + Partner, 1991), Amsterdam's Westergasfabriek Park (Gustafson Porter and Francine Houben, 1997), New York City's High Line (James Corner Field Operations and Diller, Scofidio + Renfro and Piet Oudolf,

2004), and Beringen's Play Landscape be-MINE (Carve and Omgeving, 2016). The list is extensive, starting with the very inception of landscape architecture as a profession until now. Built competitions have changed the faces of the cities we live in, established landscape architecture as a practice and profession, and continue to expand the field.

Award-winning projects also give much needed visibility to the still largely invisible and misunderstood breadth of the landscape architecture profession. Over one million people a year visit Landshaftspark and an estimated eight million visit the High Line annually. In addition to visitor numbers, successful projects are published in a wide variety of print and digital media and are discussed, debated, and used as case studies in environmental design programs across the globe. Once in a while, controversial non-winners also work their way into the public and academic conversations, such as the Parc de la Villette proposal by Rem Koolhaas and team. Koolhaas's articulation of programmatic "congestion" and design as a method instead of a thing has boldly claimed space in architecture, landscape, and urban design history and theory discourse. The competition entry is a prime example of speculation at its best – the representation of ideas in text, drawings, and models can set forth a provocative manifesto. In this instance, Koolhaas lost but also won, as have we.

Winning and losing are inseparable from the design competition. But power and fear can be taken out of the binary scenario by realizing the complexity and space in between where making happens, paradigms shift, stances emerge, collaborations form, and ideas grow. I urge you to take a walk for the sake of walking and enter a design competition for the joy and stimulation of the creative process. Hell, even smoke a cigarette if you feel like it, or raise your glass and make a toast to your brave design experiments. We certainly need all of the joy, defibrillating interruptions, skill, originality, and collaborative partnerships we can forge in this increasingly mad world.

1 Billy Collis, *The Art of Drowning* (University of Pittsburgh Press, 1995), 22.

2 Author interview with Walter Hood (July 28, 2022).

3 James Corner, "Projection and Disclosure in Drawing," *Landscape Architecture Magazine* 83, no. 5 (1993): 64–66.

4 Gabriel Raab-Faber, "A Message from Locusts," https://vimeo.com/user103191754.

5 Author interview with Henri Bava (July 18, 2022).

6 Author interview with Kate Orff (July 19, 2022).

7 Richard Weller, "Winning and Losing," in B. Cannon Ivers (ed.), *250 Things a Landscape Architect Should Know* (Birkhauser, 2021), 230.

THE JURY:

UNINTERRUPTED

RANIA GHOSN

JASON HO

FIONA RABY

MARK RAGGATT

MARTIN REIN-CANO

Rania Ghosn is associate professor of architecture and urbanism at MIT and founding partner of Design Earth with El Hadi Jazairy. Her practice engages the speculative design project to make visible and public the geographies of the climate crisis and her work has been exhibited widely, including at the Venice Architecture Biennale, the Bauhaus Museum Dessau, the Triennale di Milano, and the Seoul Biennale of Architecture and Urbanism. It is also featured in the permanent collection of the Museum of Modern Art in New York. Rania is founding editor of *New Geographies* and editor of *Landscapes of Energy* (2009) and coauthor of *Geographies of Trash* (2015), *Geostories: Another Architecture for the Environment* (2020), and *The Planet After Geoengineering* (2021). Rania is recipient of the Architectural League Prize (2016).

Jason Zhisen Ho is a curator, urbanist, and educator based in Guangzhou, China. He is founder of Mapping Workshop China and director of FEI Arts Museum in Guangzhou. Jason has participated in many international exhibitions including the Venice Architecture Biennale, and the Seoul Biennale of Architecture and Urbanism. He was sub-curator of the 2017 Shenzhen & Hong Kong Architecture/Urbanism Bio-City Biennale, academic convener of 2017 Guangzhou Art Week, and co-curator of the 2021 OCAT Shenzhen Biennale. Jason is an adjunct professor in the School of Architecture and Urban Design at RMIT University, Melbourne, Australia, and associate professor in the School of Architecture at South China University of Technology, Guangzhou. In 2019, he was named by China's Southern Metropolis Daily newspaper as "Star of the Year."

Fiona Raby is partner in the design studio Dunne & Raby, co-director of the Designed Realities Studio, and professor of design and social inquiry at the New School in New York City. She was chair and professor of industrial design (ID2) at Universität für angewandte Kunst in Vienna from 2011–2015 and a Reader in Design Interactions at the Royal College of Art, London from 1995. Fiona is coauthor, with Anthony Dunne, of *Design Noir: The Secret Life of Electronic Objects* (2001, 2021) and *Speculative Everything: Design, Fiction and Social Dreaming* (2013). Dunne & Raby's work has been exhibited at MoMA in New York, the Pompidou Centre in Paris, the Design Museum in London, and is in several permanent collections including MoMA, the Victoria and Albert Museum, and the Austrian Museum of Applied Arts. Dunne & Raby received the inaugural MIT Media Lab Award in 2015.

Mark Raggatt is director of the Australian design firm ARM Architecture. ARM is defiantly and zealously dedicated to the dissemination of ideas in and through architecture, and Mark's work has been described as "a delirious mash-up of influences, sources, experiments, scribbles, rantings, critical writings, interviews, essays and major projects, all piled one on top of the other." His award-winning design work includes the University of Sydney College of the Arts and the Gold Coast HoTA Outdoor Stage, and he is currently working on the Sydney Opera House renewal. Coeditor of *Mongrel Rapture: The Architecture of Ashton Raggatt McDougall*, Mark continues his research and teaching through the Masters of Architecture programs at RMIT University in Melbourne and the University of Technology Sydney. His current research is focused on the role of design and designer in reconciliation and decolonization of the built environment in Australia.

Martin Rein-Cano is founder and creative director of the award-winning Berlin-based design firm TOPOTEK 1. Hailing from Buenos Aires, Martin studied art history and landscape architecture in Germany before founding TOPOTEK 1 in 1999. Working at the intersection of the fields of landscape architecture, urbanism, and architecture, TOPOTEK 1's designs explore the fringes of typologies and scales, using strategies such as the recontextualization of objects and scenographic sequencing to challenge and engage the user. Its work has been widely exhibited and written about, and has received many prestigious awards including the Aga Khan Award for Architecture 2016 for Superkilen in Copenhagen; the Qatar Sustainability Awards 2018 for the Novy Arbat project in Moscow, the German Landscape architecture Prize 2015 for the UNESCO World Heritage Site Cloister Lorsch in Germany, and the FIABCI 2017 Prix d'Excellence Germany Gold Prize. Martin is a visiting professor at Dessau Institute for Architecture and a veteran of many design competition juries.

+ What are your general impressions of the "interruptions" you reviewed? What was of most interest to you and why?

Rania Ghosn As I reviewed the entries the words of French philosopher Jacques Rancière–*Move along! There is nothing to see*–were resonating in my head, perhaps more so because one of the entries brought him up in their text. These words illustrate how the organization of space–and in particular the "space of flows"–operates toward the consolidation of a disciplinary policing order – of what constitutes a design question, how to respond to it and through which aesthetics. What is common to all such disciplining projects is the impossibility of the witness–of the person who stands still and sees an event, typically a crime or accident, take place–and is required to produce a sensible account, or forms of evidence and proof. While the space of flows requires protestors to clear the streets, to move along, the act of standing, of interrupting flows, refigures what there is to do, what there is to see or to name. Design consists of transforming the space of circulation into a space for the manifestation of a subject. It resists the closure of categories of thought and of the aesthetic project with which to think and speak to multiple possible meanings.

Interruption is the rupture of some normal(ized) distribution of roles, places, and occupations in a specific geography and the subsequent manifestation of dissensus within it. The witness looks precisely into where "there is nothing to see" – and this is the power of interruption and of this competition. The most memorable submissions have identified that which makes them pause, made the harmful visible, and responded with a speculative proposal of form and reform. If you see something, design something. "Interruption" was an impressive manifestation of the ways in which design can disrupt the closure of spatial sites and symbols and can interrogate the construction of solid spatial concepts, representations, and fixed subject positions. Competition entries addressed the climate crisis in terms of air pollution, oil extraction sites, energy production, and integrated technologies–whether preexisting or emerging–to revisit the symbolism of the design project at urban and territorial scales. These projects are fundamentally political because they disturb the consensual order of solidified categories by opening design to current spatial crises – of climate, democracy, labor, trauma. To paraphrase Rancière, design is "a dispute about the division of what is perceptible to the senses."

Jason Ho I felt that a large portion of the "interruptions" relied on spatial transformation from the overarching perspective of God and the profession of landscape architecture. The scale of selected sites was generally quite large and the intensity of the interruptions rather strong.

I am more interested in projects that respond to current socio-political issues at a smaller scale – ones that address issues spatially, but which might also trigger positive cognitive or behavioral changes in the people that use those spaces. Often these are artistic interruptions that may be offensive, radical, uncomfortable, and ironic, while still being enlightening for the community. Interruptions with social agendas require bold imagination and critical thinking. Working at a smaller scale brings modesty, humility, and precision. These artistic expressions–as well as the social justice and public values conveyed by these expressions–are what today's landscape architects need to be good at.

 Fiona Raby

I always like to see projects that challenge expectations – propositions that allow us to rethink deeply engrained assumptions, even if we know they are unlikely to be realized. There were quite a few of those, however, the Manhattan Curtain project did leap out in its audacity, I had to smile imagining such a brutal structure cutting across Manhattan. Deliberately "unreal," it manages to highlight the current proliferation of underlying values, showing us exactly what kinds of extremes might be needed to reach targets that are politically ignored – complete with a tremendous new viewing platform for the city.

But perhaps personally and more importantly for me are projects that evoke sensuality and immersion in complex natural ecologies. Even what might seem simple—an undoing or undesigning—could lead us into lush, rich, nonhuman-centered environments; for example, the regeneration of mangrove swamps. How do we interrupt the relentless human "progress," which only considers habitats and solutions for one species above all else. I realize that this was the theme of the LA+ CREATURE competition, but I do think we need many more of these kinds of interruptions. A few projects this year were critical of failed political schemes – for example, a rural market structure built in the name of economic and global progress, sitting empty and unused. Instead, abandonment and rewilding were offered as more accurate and "realistic" propositions – a counterpoint to tired political and economic claims. Other schemes would emerge over decades, planned meticulously, as suggested in the rewilding of Milan – forests would grow where once there were cars and roads; but this is not a human-centered rewilding, here the rewilding is explicitly to the exclusion of humans. I absolutely love this. Is it possible to create spaces that are not for our enjoyment?

As I take pleasure in this impossibility, in the human-centered world, an article arrives on my screen. I read about a Dutch town transformed with 1,000 trees, described as a "walking" forest – part of an art festival, where trees in enormous plant pots were temporarily wheeled in on large wagons by volunteers over many months. It was staged deliberately as a spectacle, complete with QR codes to make sure the trees could be identified, regularly watered, and looked after. The transformation was so profound, cooling the hot, previously trafficked streets, the locals asked, "Why didn't we have trees there before?" And I love this too. Something, so needed, so obvious, so possible, yet politically so impossible to achieve through official channels, just gets done through individuals and collective willpower. Although only temporary, another reality was enabled and experienced. A desire for something different has been instilled.

Within a milieu of multiple crises and urgency, it's very hard to imagine spaces of joy, of joyfulness, so I am a little old fashioned, I love to see projects that even in their intense criticality, are still materially rich, sensual propositions, vivid, and celebratory.

 Mark Raggatt

There is a sense that the current world order, its power structures, and its economic assumptions are failing. There is a sense that the environment is speaking back to us, a once small voice now shouting an interruption to the industrious path we set. The entrants seem to have heard that call. This is important for the designers of the built environment – we have an opportunity to answer that voice, to amplify it, and to add our own in support. There is an argument to be one–for deniers to be convinced– and this gives us a responsibility, a role in providing shape and strategy for a kinder Anthropocene.

The interruptions we might once have expected from such a competition would have been self-consciously avant-garde, but I think that might be an inaccurate way to assess this competition, a now inappropriate orthodoxy. Rather, these interruptions were visions of a return to order, almost a return to Eden lost. These entries seemed to seek an interruption to the chaos of human consumption, the chaos we have introduced, the ecosystems we have interrupted, the interrupted communities we have divided, and the interrupted minds we have conjured for ourselves. The interruption of this competition seems to me to be a reinstatement of the complex ecological balance. In that, I thought these entries were hopeful without being optimistic.

Simultaneously, there seemed to be a return to humanism, human experience, and interaction as something to take joy in – not as consumers but as citizens. Empathy isn't something we reference enough when we talk about the built environment. When we interact with our cities and with other citizens through our built environment we can encourage empathy or conversely manufacture enmity. What does an empathic city look like, anyway?

Martin Rein-Cano

I was impressed by the diversity within the collection of entries. There was a wide range of concepts and ideas, from the highly imaginary to the most detailed, specific, and tangible proposals. More than a few triggered my interest and provoked thoughtful discussions. But actually, it was more the abstract ideas and conceptual approaches that stood out and caught my attention. I am continually inspired by how, through them, we can consider and develop new directions to create better places in our shared environments without necessarily having to be detailed and explicit.

+ What would you have done, or at least what sort of direction would have you taken had you entered this competition? What needs to be interrupted these days?

Rania Ghosn

It is a very open prompt, which I find difficult, not least that the site is open – and for my practice, geographic situatedness is key. I probably would have extended the series of projects on animal figures rebelling against the natural history museum-institutions that house their skeletons or taxidermies. These mascot figures break the silence and stillness of the museum setup, itself sometimes complicit with fossil fuel interests. The first of the series was Elephant in the Room and we are currently working on Whale in the Room. These short animations have a Dr Seuss quality to them, in that they extend the audience of the design project to a broader cultural audience. In that sense, its ultimate interruption is that of the closed world of design readership and audience.

Jason Ho For me, the act of interruption is akin to the act of acupuncture in traditional Chinese medicine. Therefore, my approach would be to find the most effective "acupoints" without changing the original characteristics and structures of the site, and in that way enable the most effective changes in urban public space with minimum intensity.

In China, the original urban landscape has been completely changed by large-scale demolition and construction in the past three decades. Designers are used to looking at cities in plan view from above, but this means that important small details are often ignored. From my perspective, an ideal interruption would look at very specific sites from a worm's-eye view, taking the existing patterns of site use as a point of departure in achieving maximum effect with minimum intervention. A small-scale interruption might not affect the whole city, but it can enrich the environment. The interruption is an accretional approach, where small changes accumulate to transform situations that can eventually affect the larger urban landscape.

Fiona Raby Human dominance is under examination. Anything around the nonhuman, inter-species ecologies, decentering the human, and the Post Humanities has exploded recently as a counterpoint to sustainability, highlighting a very different set of knotty contradictory and complex challenges. But when it comes down to it and we sit down together with our students to imagine these other worlds or ways of being in the world, there is a quick realization of the impossibility to step out of the human frame: we can never experience what it is like to be another creature or take the perspective of a plant and think for them, it's riddled with complexity and contradiction. It's a wonderful dilemma, an exercise that requires humility, stretching the imagination, and some very unusual creative design tactics. Ultimately it clearly reveals the responsibilities carried by the human species.

Mark Raggatt Architecture seems predetermined to be complicit, to be conservative, and to be nostalgic. At times like these with global unrest in the shape of climate change, disease, regime change, and revolutions in race and gender equality, architecture seems to be retreating toward nostalgia and good taste. I can't tell if this is because we lack the tools to communicate the current age, if architecture is too anachronistic to cope with the pace of change, or if we just prefer the safety of things tried and tested. I don't know if we prefer our roles as professional aesthetes or complicit technocrats to the powerful. I suspect that we are optimistic and hope that if we do the right thing, someone will notice. I think this is misguided.

In Australia and in other parts of the world where colonizers attempted to displace first peoples, we are necessarily beginning to understand the lessons of traditional custodians. These lessons, if taken seriously, interrupt the discipline of architecture in fundamental ways – in ways that undermine the foundations of our discipline, which is founded on precedent and a hoped-for permanence. Response to "context" is a fine example. If in a colonial city there are say, lots of arches (as there are in Sydney where I live and work), is it appropriate to affirm that built environment and cultural history when it represents the colonization and attempted genocide of the oldest continuous culture on earth? If it is not appropriate, then how do we recalibrate our understanding of architectural design, city planning, and urban history? We need to interrupt the snoozy smugness of contemporary architecture. The discipline itself has uncomfortable questions to face; this interruption to our complicit nostalgia could contribute to the reconciliation of peoples and in the process perhaps prove ourselves worthy of the forgiveness and grace we have already received.

Martin Rein-Cano

I would interrupt the interruption, that being the traditional conception of landscape architecture that works to balance, decelerate, and remediate the flow. Rather than interrupting the flow, I would be interested in using its velocity and our increasing knowledge of nature and its dialectic qualities to integrate and embed diversity and dynamism within the project. This means allowing for the ambiguity and fluidity of identity – not just of people, but also of plants and everyday objects found or discovered outside of their expected contexts. Landscape architecture in urban contexts historically has tried to create order, peace, and harmony – in other words, perfection. But good urban spaces need a certain degree of conflict, because as I see it, a sense of danger awakens our senses. Spaces of divergence, ambiguity, and translation generate social encounters that, to some extent, can vaccinate against larger battles. So many contemporary landscape projects that "interrupt" through pacification miss out on the potential in aestheticizing conflict. They do not allow for conflicts to run their course or, more importantly, to be translated. Translation occurs, for example, when a fist fight in one context is considered assault but in another context–say, a boxing ring–it is considered good physical exercise and a spectator sport. The practice of interruption should take lessons from the freedom of artistic strategies, often through which the zeitgeist is continuously challenged and where the most brilliant pieces emerge from an infidelity to conventional desires.

In your practice Design Earth (with El Hadi Jazairy) you produce visuals that speak to the dominant technological narratives of contemporary culture. Could you explain how this project sits within the broader discourses of the Capitalocene, and what you see as the role of designers in this new, climate-changed context?

RANIA GHOSN

Design Earth explores speculative architectural projects as narrative devices for tackling environmental and climatic concerns. This form of practice is particularly relevant because the discipline is entrenched in but not always sensible to the politics of extraction and pollution. Design Earth started from a discontent with what goes unnoticed in the design professions or is taken for granted, namely the material flows, energy networks, and technological infrastructures that form the backbone of our homes and cities and make them function.

In response to this lack of acknowledgment, we investigate the technologies and processes behind waste management, fossil fuel extraction, rare earth mining, carbon storage, space missions, and more, to make visible their role in transforming our environment. And our designs do not stop short at the immediate urban environment, but extend their scope far beyond to other planetary scales and territories–below the ground, at the bottom of the ocean, up in the sky, and in outer space–based on the recognition that the externalities of these technologies are distributed across the planet, its geological strata, and its atmosphere. We think, as we discuss in *Geostories: Another Architecture for the Environment*, that climate change is not only a crisis of the physical environment, but also a crisis of the cultural environment and of the systems of representation through which we make sense of our presence on the planet. Taking stock of the planet's ongoing transformation, Design Earth offers a possible reappropriation of the imagination: a profoundly spatialized task. These cautionary tales for the Anthropocene are undoubtedly worlds apart from the bright future visions commonly proposed by architecture, and yet, as we will see, they are hopeful in that they start developing an understanding of what it means to care for the planet and encourage a conversation about the world we would like to inhabit tomorrow.

JASON HO

Because rather than providing design services to big development you do small-scale installations and events that are deeply embedded in local culture, your work in China seems non-conformist. Each of your projects seems like a small but precise "interruption" in the symbolic order of things. What do you think designers can take from this mode of practice?

I like to understand the local culture first before I start an interruption in a place. The cultural practice of a place in China plays a very important role in determining how landscape architects should approach the design or redesign of a site. Landscape architects have to understand how Chinese people use and read spaces in their everyday lives before they start making new rules and regulations and imposing big forms. For example, in China people like to appropriate public space. The boundary between public and private is much more porous and blurred than that in a Western context. A public space can be easily transformed into a personal space through such appropriations.

Street-vending, for example, is such a phenomenon in China. We cannot deny that it is part of our culture. The moment a street vendor puts the props on the ground, he or she is drawing a personal boundary to create a new commercial space. When the vendor is gone, the boundary disappears and another type of informal occupation takes over. This type of ephemeral occupation of space can never be captured in a bird's-eye view or through a top-down model. Designers rarely anticipate designing for street vendors, but through knowing how they will use a site designers can make more effective and simple micro-infrastructures.

Public spaces in Chinese cities are generally not designed with any degree of intimacy. They are enormous, super neat, highly controlled, and well programmed, but they are barely used and left empty most of the time. How could landscape architects start making interruptions or even destroying the established orders that exist in those symbolic landscapes? My approach is to be open to the chaos of life. Chaos is not a problem – under the right conditions it self-organizes and new, more complex forms of order emerge. There is always an order within chaos. As landscape architects we need to find this deeper order behind the appearance of chaotic phenomenon and work with it, not against it.

FIONA RABY

Your work in partnership with Anthony Dunne is well known under the rubric of speculative design, which you have described as shifting design's focus away from commercial expediency on the one hand and problem solving on the other. In many ways, then, speculative design can be understood as something of an interruption to the status quo. Tell us about what you are currently working on or thinking about in this regard.

As object designers we tend to challenge the status quo through the existence of very different kinds of objects. We never limit ourselves to an existing palette and prefer to invent and introduce new typologies and ask the viewer: Why can't we have objects like these? Why don't they exist in the world? Why are they deemed impossible or unrealistic?

To understand this further we are making an archive of impossible objects with one section focusing on decentering the human and all the contradictions, desires, and dilemmas that arise through this endeavor. This part of the project has come out of a long-term fascination with wilderness – since we have lived in America we have been back-country camping in remote areas, entering nonhuman habitats with the mindset of treading lightly and "leaving no trace." In these spaces our experience of humanness has been reduced to humble biomass. We want to interrupt by acknowledging complexity, challenging divisive thinking, making sure subtle nuance and all those rich precious quirky bits don't get ironed out, particularly if they don't quite fit so well. The awkward and the esoteric is also part of everyday life.

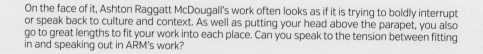

MARK RAGGATT

On the face of it, Ashton Raggatt McDougall's work often looks as if it is trying to boldly interrupt or speak back to culture and context. As well as putting your head above the parapet, you also go to great lengths to fit your work into each place. Can you speak to the tension between fitting in and speaking out in ARM's work?

We are always just trying to fit in. Maybe the tension you describe is like that in 1828 when Heinrich Hubsch asked, "In what style should we build?" – the vexed hand-wringing question of an appropriate style for a client, building type, nation, or zeitgeist. That question is testing validity, approval, and appropriateness. It tests self-worth, expression, localness, cringe, climate, and innovation. In what style do we find a style?

ARM does not have a style – not in the sense that we have characteristic gestures that define our practice, but we do have a Style in the sense of a method, a way of doing and thinking, a way of understanding. That method is to begin with not knowing, to begin with questioning, not affecting answers but beginning as if from scratch. I am thinking of the Barak Tower in Melbourne, a multi-residential development on the edge of Melbourne's CBD. It has 500 apartments and the face of William Barak (1824–1903)– the last traditional aboriginal elder of Melbourne's Wurundjeri people—as its façade. The building is questioning, reflecting, and speculating all at once. It requires knowledge of who that face represents to apprehend what possible meaning it might convey, but as we get closer to it that meaning seems to evaporate into just more questions.

When we are at our best, we find ways for architecture to capture an intensely local culture and, we hope, something of human history and experience, too. Maybe that's what makes it seem as if we're speaking out when we're just reflecting what we see, maybe it's the reflection that speaks like a conscience and the process of reflecting that is uncomfortable.

TOPOTEK 1's work is well known and admired because instead of aiming only for pacification and respite through the beauty of "nature," you seek out and work with tension, contradiction, and even forms of conflict in your projects. Through this—as projects like Superkilen in Copenhagen show—you have been able to interrupt the stranglehold that 18th-century landscape aesthetics has on landscape architecture. How do you maintain this approach in projects where clients and the community have applied pressure for a more conventional image of landscape and insist on environmental performance as a priority?

MARTIN REIN-CANO

Our projects are only ever as good as the quality of the collaboration between designers, clients, and other partners, both within and outside the studio. Meaningful collaborations necessitate approaches that strive for initiative, communication, and activity between people. It enables the crossing over of disciplines and ideologies which in turn leads to the discovery of new hybrids and opportunities. Capturing the momentum of good collaborations can transform any design potential into a positive and impactful force. This is because strong, animated relationships between stakeholders lead to compelling creations that would otherwise not arise out of purely rational thinking or unilateral design. At the same time, we have a passion at TOPOTEK 1 for challenging prescriptive functionality and single use of space. This is especially relevant when it comes to the environmental performance of projects with important sustainability criteria to be met; for example, area storm water retention. It is here that we need to do the convincing work of saying, "look, a car is not just a carriage without horses, it is a distinct entity with entirely new programmatic potential." The same applies to the environmental performance features that we are more and more required to incorporate within our design projects. Instead of addressing the requirements as challenges, we work through our collaborations to discover new typologies and new hybrid uses that can be synthesized from these features. A good example of this would be our master plan for Downtown Høje Taastrup, where the storm water retention swale—which is only filled after exceptionally heavy rainfall that is more and more frequent with climate change—is also a continuous skate bowl. In this way, our design work has interrupted the pervasive social preoccupation with climate change by allowing for special moments to also occur between intense weather events. The success is not so much about maintaining a specific approach on all projects, but rather about exploiting the latent creative energy that exists automatically when you mix new collaborators in a new context.

WINNERS

XIANGYU LIU CHENGXI ZHA CENGYUAN XU

NEW YORK, NEW YORK
UNITED STATES

In the complex environment of Manhattan, the air stream carries a variety of impure gasses: byproducts from industry, building air conditioning and heating systems, and vehicle exhausts. In order to successfully reach the goal of 80% carbon emission reduction in Manhattan by 2050, the idea for the Manhattan Curtain was born.

Carbon Capture, Utilization, and Storage technology (CCUS) captures and purifies the CO_2 emissions and subsequently puts it into a new process that allows the CO_2 to be recycled rather than sequestered. The Manhattan Curtain is an architectural practice based on CCUS technology at an urban scale. The project starts with 630 carbon dioxide-filter membranes. Amine compounds are attached to filters to absorb carbon dioxide and chemically convert it into carbide. The carbide is then transported to the CCUS towers on either side of the Curtain. After multiple filtering and decomposition processes, it is ultimately transformed into industrial products such as baking soda and biodegradable plastics, aiming for efficient and clean green applications of carbon-based energy.

The filters hang from trusses suspended between the CCUS towers, forming a giant curtain on W 59th St – physically interrupting the gray skyscrapers and the green Central Park. As well as capturing and processing the vast carbon emissions from Midtown and Downtown, the towers also enrich city life by allowing citizens to enter the interior to learn about purifying the air, and to stand at a new high point with a great view of Manhattan. Aesthetically, the filter Curtain has a colorful, stained window-like effect. The Manhattan Curtain is a monument to the barbarically grown city with the highest density of high-rise buildings in human history, interrupting the status quo and symbolizing the city's move to a sustainable future.

MANHATTAN CURTAIN

Interruption 1

CO2 ← CCUS → Manhattan

Manhattan Curtain

Midtown ← Giant Installation   Monument → Gray City

Interruption 2

Central Park

Interruption 3

Green Architecture

CCUS Tower System

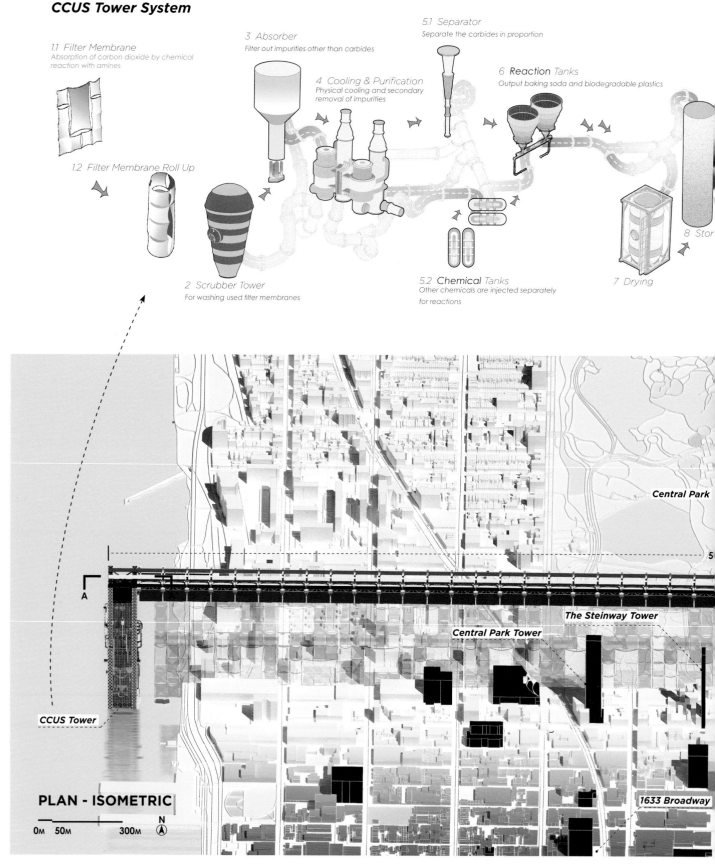

1.1 Filter Membrane
Absorption of carbon dioxide by chemical reaction with amines

3 Absorber
Filter out impurities other than carbides

5.1 Separator
Separate the carbides in proportion

4 Cooling & Purification
Physical cooling and secondary removal of impurities

6 Reaction Tanks
Output baking soda and biodegradable plastics

1.2 Filter Membrane Roll Up

2 Scrubber Tower
For washing used filter membranes

5.2 Chemical Tanks
Other chemicals are injected separately for reactions

7 Drying

8 Stor

Central Park

The Steinway Tower

Central Park Tower

CCUS Tower

1633 Broadway

PLAN - ISOMETRIC

0M 50M 300M N

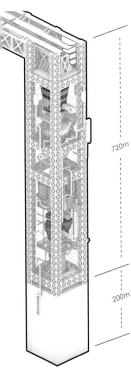

720m

200m

CCUS Tower

Truss Structures

Manhattan Curtain

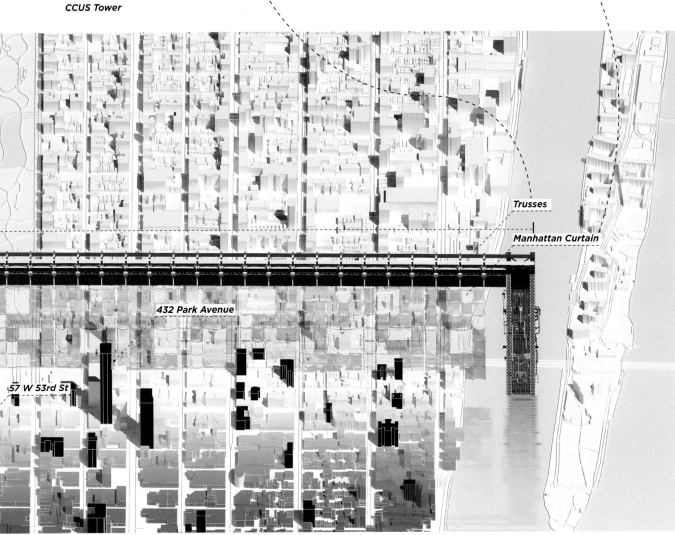

Trusses

Manhattan Curtain

432 Park Avenue

57 W 53rd St

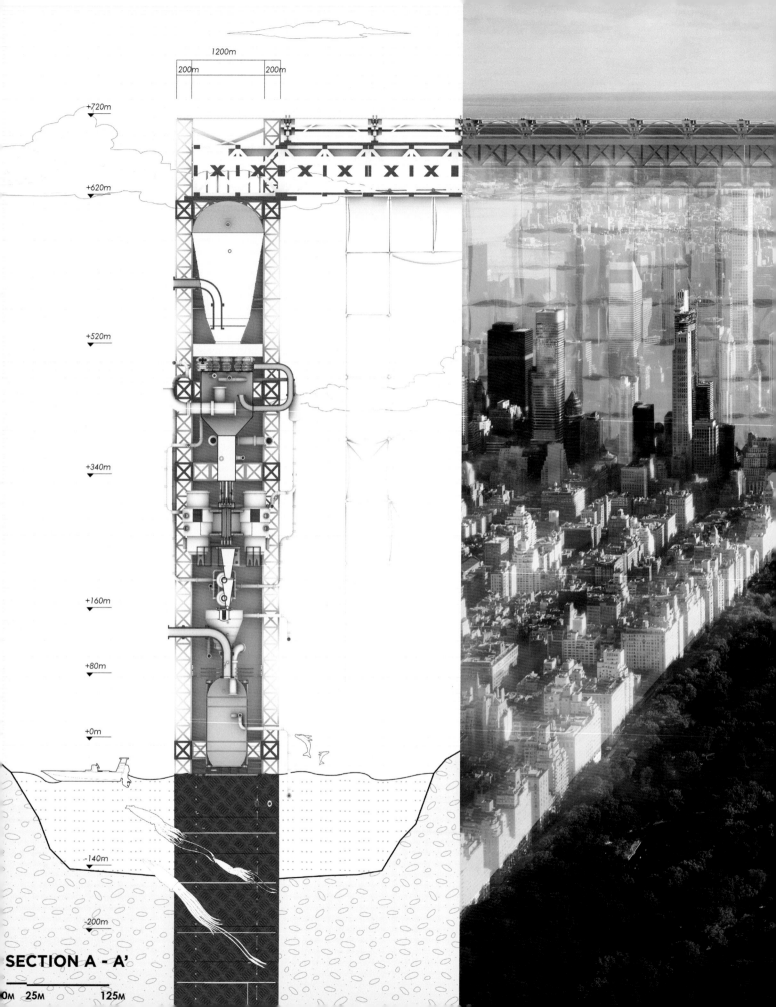

SECTION A - A'

0M 25M   125M

JAKE BOSWELL

PITTSBURGH, PENNSYLVANIA
UNITED STATES

A dam is a literal interruption. According to the National Inventory of Dams, there are over 90,000 dams in the US. Less than 2% of these generate hydroelectric power. Many of the other 98% do essential work, yet their potential as an energy source is unrealized. This project shows one way to harness the energy embodied in these dams.

River Prosthesis 1 takes the Emsworth Dam on the Ohio River near Pittsburgh, Pennsylvania, as a test case. Emsworth is a 25' lift-gate dam that allows navigation to Pittsburgh and up the Allegheny and Monongahela rivers. The project deploys three pre-existing technologies: a hydraulic ram pump, a water tower, and a water turbine to create a prosthetic infrastructure, converting the existing dam into a hydro-power plant and a pumped-hydro storage battery. In so doing, it creates a second, more speculative interruption.

Contemporary discussions of renewable energy assume that ample chemical battery storage can balance wind and solar output variability. That assumption is crazy. Already we cannot mine lithium-carbonate quickly enough to keep up with the demand for electric car batteries. How will we produce enough to power our homes and cities (let alone quickly)? Currently, 95% of the world's energy storage comes from pumped hydro. These facilities use excess energy at times of low demand to pump water to elevated reservoirs. Water is released through a turbine when demand is high to balance shortfalls in production. Traditionally, pumped hydro has been land consumptive, but it is also cheap, safe, and reliable. Increased rainfall projected for the Upper Midwest, East, and Southeast makes pumped hydro facilities even more feasible.

As global temperatures rise, cities are increasingly susceptible to extreme heat events. During such events, energy demand skyrockets. As demand outstrips production, we will see rolling blackouts. River Prosthesis can help balance out normal variability while also powering a reliable, redundantly distributed, zero-carbon micro-grid, ensuring that critical infrastructures like cooling centers and hospitals can continue to function.

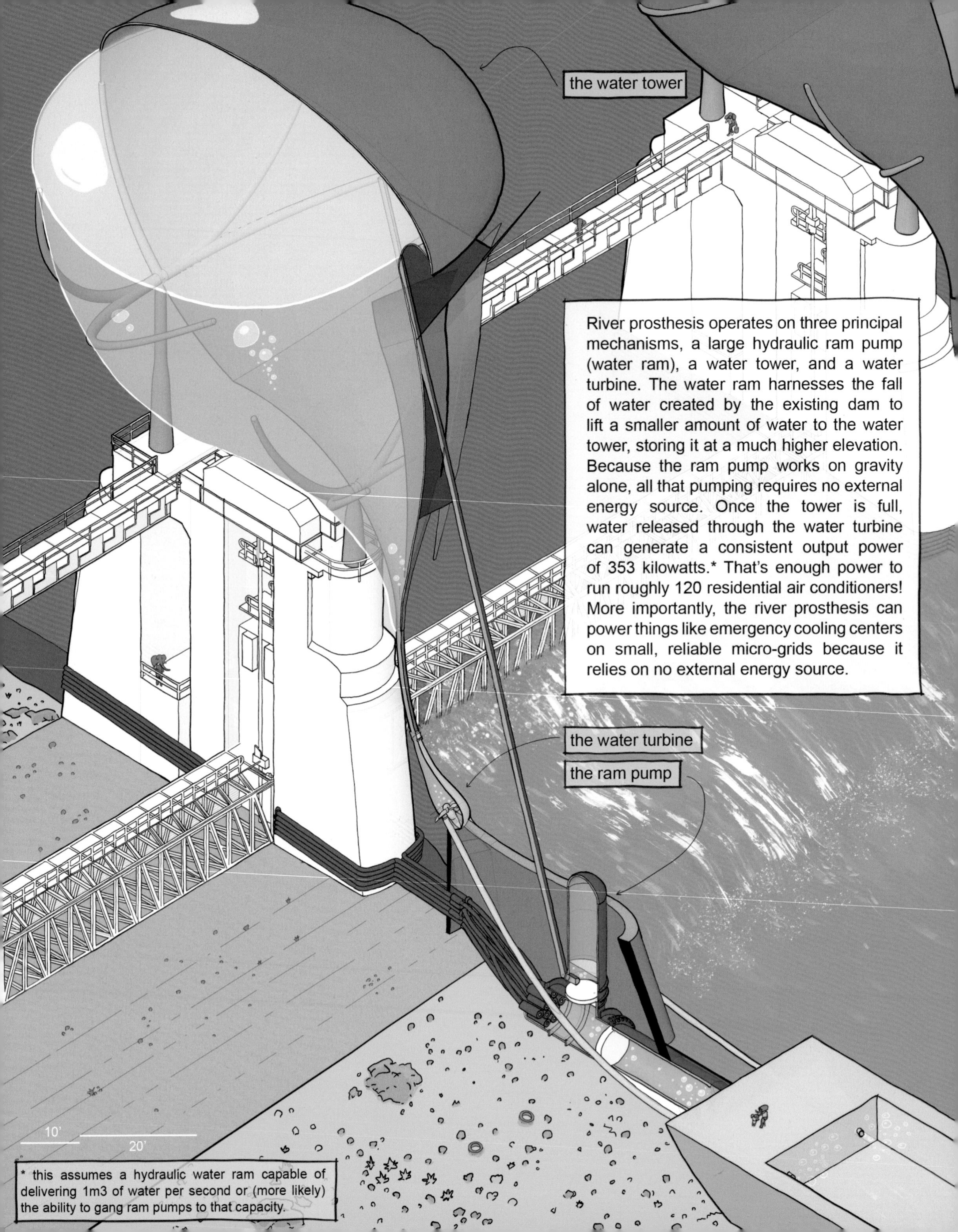

the water tower

River prosthesis operates on three principal mechanisms, a large hydraulic ram pump (water ram), a water tower, and a water turbine. The water ram harnesses the fall of water created by the existing dam to lift a smaller amount of water to the water tower, storing it at a much higher elevation. Because the ram pump works on gravity alone, all that pumping requires no external energy source. Once the tower is full, water released through the water turbine can generate a consistent output power of 353 kilowatts.* That's enough power to run roughly 120 residential air conditioners! More importantly, the river prosthesis can power things like emergency cooling centers on small, reliable micro-grids because it relies on no external energy source.

the water turbine

the ram pump

10'

20'

* this assumes a hydraulic water ram capable of delivering 1m3 of water per second or (more likely) the ability to gang ram pumps to that capacity.

Because it stores water at a high elevation, the water tower can act as a kinetic battery. When full, the water tower contains 930-kilowatt hours of potential energy. This stored energy can be used in a "peaking" capacity when local energy demand is high, much like a typical pumped hydro facility, to balance shortfalls from more intermittent energy sources like solar and wind. In a large river like the Ohio, a pumped storage facility like this could operate continuously, producing and storing energy as needed.

An outfall chamber captures water exiting the system and slows it down. Here that chamber doubles as a public in-river swimming pool.

25'

A full tower produces a continuous 353 kW of power.

During peak demand, each tower can supply .9 MW hours of electricity.

It takes 3.5 hours for the ram pump to fill the tank.

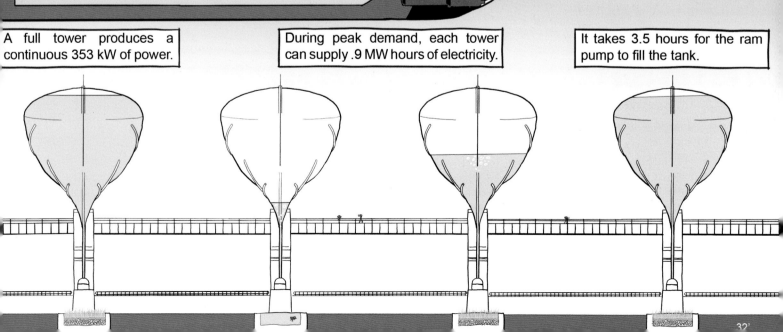

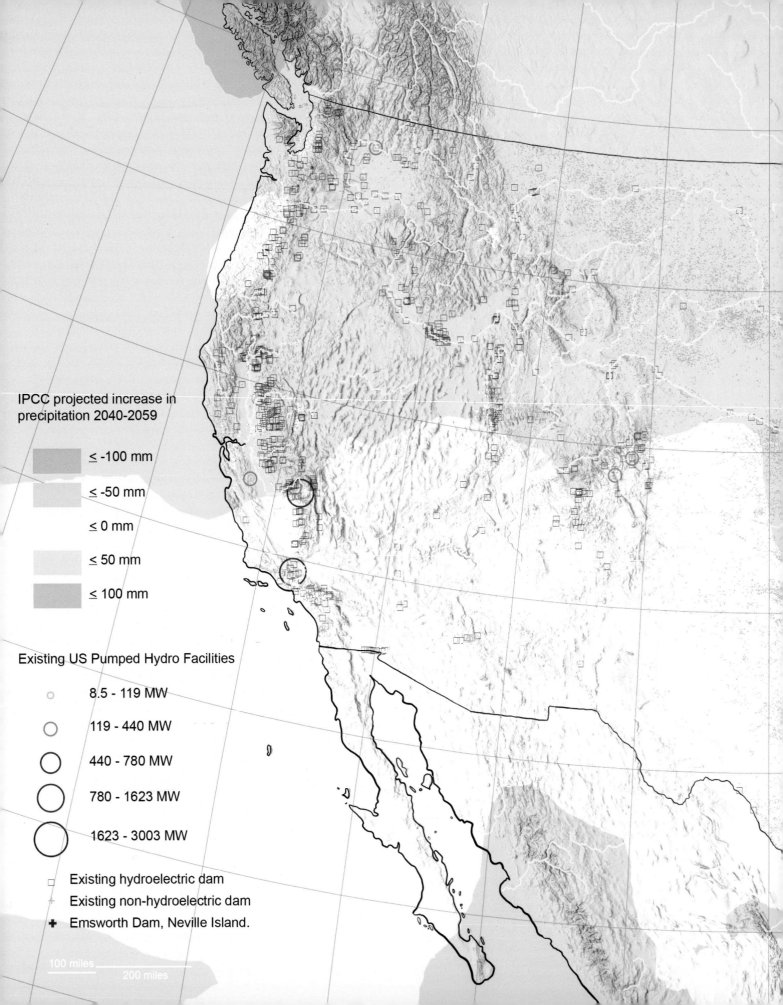

IPCC projected increase in
precipitation 2040-2059

≤ -100 mm

≤ -50 mm

≤ 0 mm

≤ 50 mm

≤ 100 mm

Existing US Pumped Hydro Facilities

○   8.5 - 119 MW

○   119 - 440 MW

○   440 - 780 MW

○   780 - 1623 MW

○   1623 - 3003 MW

□   Existing hydroelectric dam

     Existing non-hydroelectric dam

✚   Emsworth Dam, Neville Island.

100 miles
          200 miles

There are over 90,000 dams in the US. Currently, only about 2% of those dams produce hydroelectric power. As climate change increases rainfall in the upper midwest, east, and southeast, finding ways to harness potential energy embodied in those dams could become critical to maintaining a stable, carbon-free power grid.

ANTOINE APRUZZESE
THOMAS ROCHE
ANNE KLEPAL

PARIS
FRANCE

In western neoliberal societies today, we witness a crisis of representative democracy associated with the "post-politics" condition: a general depoliticization of society, a decrease of counter-powers, and disappearance of actual political debate, concomitant to increasing violence against protest movements. Democracy is often considered as the operative system ordering society, in which we vote for our representatives making laws and governing our territories. But democracy is also the process through which people become able to govern themselves. For this empowerment to happen, people need to express different opinions, confront their ideas, acknowledge how different they are, form communities, and understand that they have to work together and include minorities in decision-making processes. As Jacques Rancière stated, "there is politics precisely when one reveals as false the evidence that the community exists already and everyone is already included."

In this context, cities bear the marks of this crisis in democracy: facades are oversaturated with advertising, buildings appear as symbols of companies' power, and public places are ruled by security restrictions and surveillance. The city of Paris is still strongly influenced by its Haussmann heritage, with city streets and public places designed as a framework for shutting down any revolution. In addition, a 1981 French law made posting fliers illegal on the facades of public institutions and other public places, with a tolerance for fliers posted on scaffoldings.

There is no politics without spatial anchoring, thus spaces of public expression and debate need to be embodied and recognizable. This proposal builds upon practices of demonstration such as signs, slogans, and fliers – it deflects the existing facades by building an outdoor room made of scaffolding-inspired structures as a support for allowing opinions to be expressed, communities to emerge, and democracy to form. As a political reinterpretation of Cedric Price's Fun Palace, the interruption replaces activities with ones helping the construction of a strong public sphere, and a living democracy.

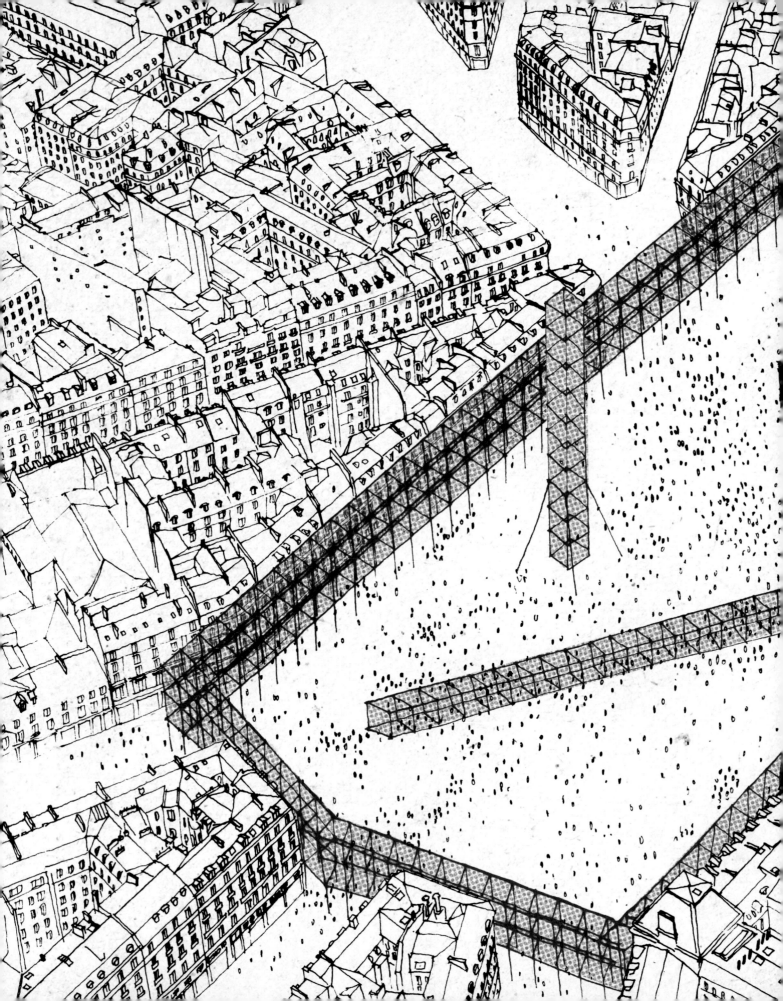

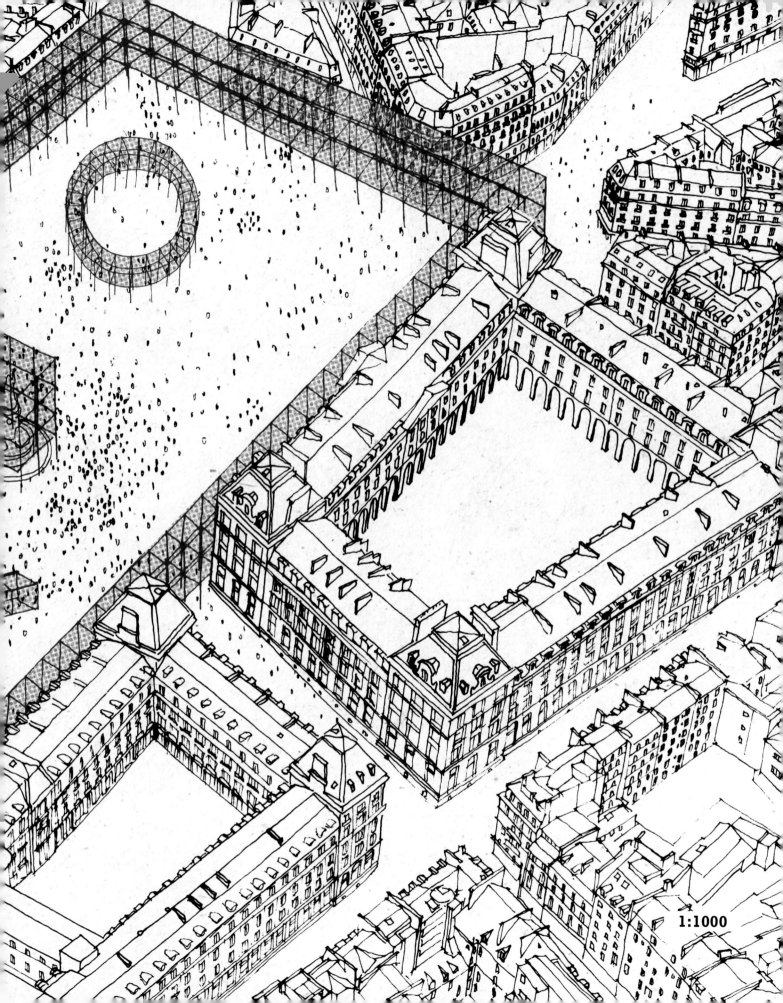

1:1000

HONORABLE MENTIONS

JOSEPH HENRY KENNEDY JR.
VINCENT PARLATORE
HANA SVATOŠ-RAŽNJEVIC

>>>>>>>> **MULTIPLE SITES — EUROPE**

The sidewalk is the site of a perpetual territorial dispute between building and street, both seeking to extend their domain into the thin space that separates them. This ambiguous territory plays host to numerous informal events that are manifestations of commercial interests and the personal needs of residents. As socioeconomic forces threaten to shrink the sidewalk into nonexistence, these narrow public realms are at risk of extinction.

As old European capitals struggle to accommodate increased vehicle traffic on their narrow streets, roads are cut through the old city fabric, displacing parks and sidewalks with the addition of extra lanes and parking spaces. But with Playcarpet the sidewalk makes a comeback – the street is reclaimed as a platform for weekly fairs, parades, and farmers markets that close off roads to make way for scheduled public events.

Like a doormat that welcomes guests into a home, Playcarpet removes the threshold separating pedestrian and motorist, defining a space which resolves their mutual occupation. By temporarily erasing the boundaries of the curb, Playcarpet extends the sidewalk into the street to reclaim the public space of the city. Moving from one European capital to the next, Playcarpet reconfigures its tiles to address different urban contexts, events, and social issues. The carpet is a graphic blueprint on which multiple occupations may occur. The actions and attitudes of the public fill the gaps between architecture and empty, neutral space in which many possible social situations may unfold. A suggestion, rather than a physical imposition, Playcarpet anticipates a response from the public with elements and furniture sourced locally.

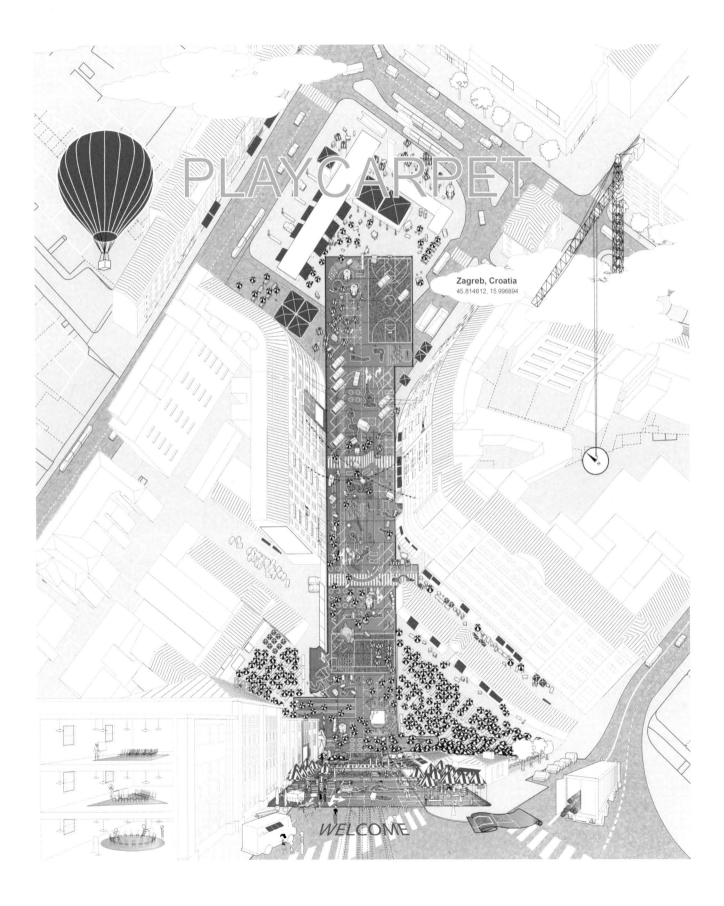

PLAYCARPET

Zagreb, Croatia
45.814612, 15.996894

WELCOME

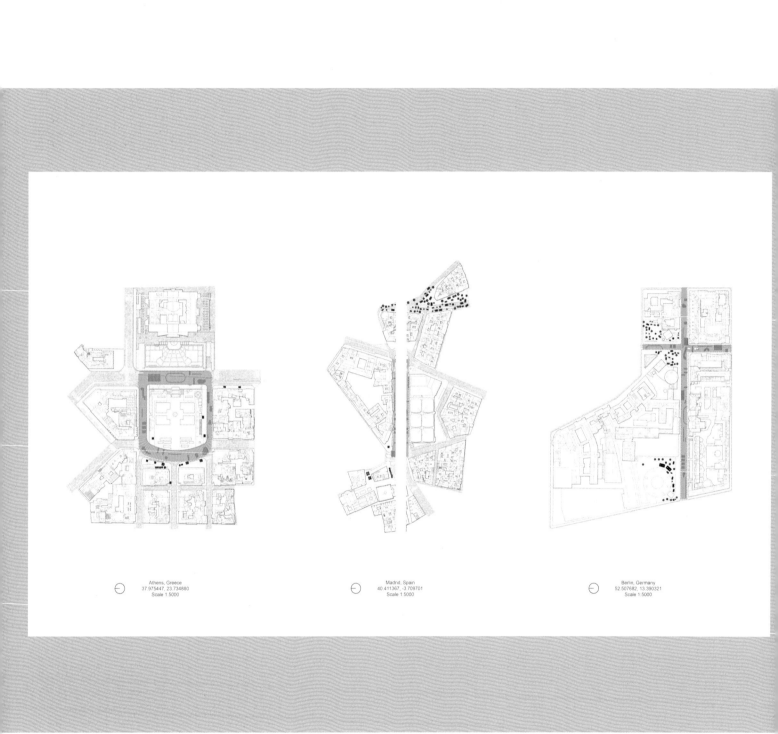

Athens, Greece
37.975447, 23.734880
Scale 1:5000

Madrid, Spain
40.411367, -3.709701
Scale 1:5000

Berlin, Germany
52.507682, 13.390321
Scale 1:5000

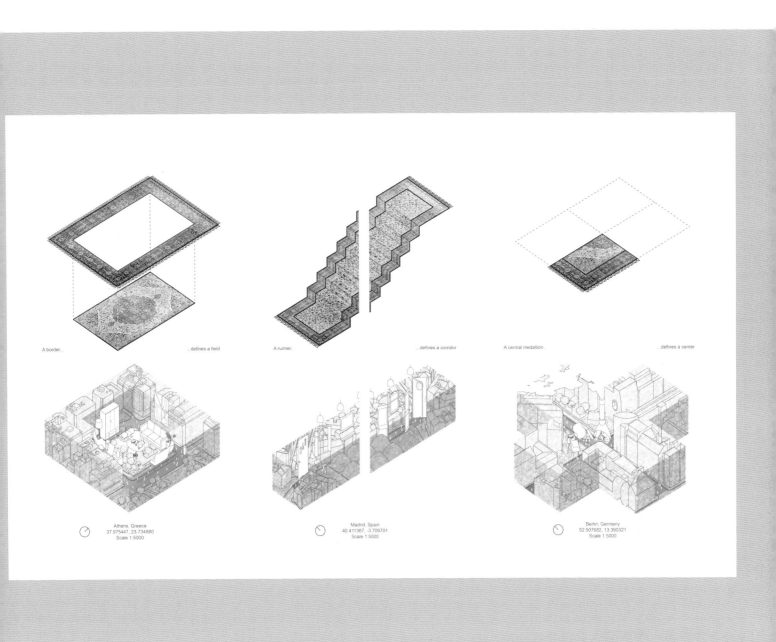

A border...   ...defines a field   A runner...   ...defines a corridor   A central medallion...   ...defines a center

Athens, Greece
37.975447, 23.734880
Scale 1:5000

Madrid, Spain
40.411367, -3.709701
Scale 1:5000

Berlin, Germany
52.507682, 13.390321
Scale 1:5000

QIUTONG HUANG
JINGJUN TAO

>>>>>>>> **CHONGQING, CHINA**

In 2021, because of a community volunteer experience with an anti-cancer kitchen, I began to pay attention to the issue of medical migration in China's urbanization process. In order to save on high hospital costs for cancer treatment, patients were required to live like an ant colony in high-density residential buildings within a radius of 500 meters of major cancer hospitals. The survival instincts of cancer patients and their families have given birth to the spontaneous formation of survival fissures within the buildings; and when we cut through the icy walls of these rental accommodations in the city, we can see the totally different life scripts of these families and the other more-permanent residents.

The design of this project is inspired by the landlord's spontaneous, and tenant's passive, spatial renovation behavior in one such building. In order to maximize economic benefits, here, a kitchen can be forced to plug 10 stovetops. The armrest gap in the stairwell is used by tenants to stretch elastic clothes lines, and they choose the most suitable drying spot for each residential building according to where the sun hits the stairwell at different times of day. What impressed me most is the fact that stand-alone wall-mounted air conditioners can be deconstructed and functionally shared via the internal walls between the two tenants. This reminded me of the Wave Function Collapse algorithm (WFC), which has become the basis for my design. In its simplest form the algorithm works on an orthogonal grid, and a set of adjacency rules describe what can occupy each tile on the grid depending on what its neighbors are. The grid tiles are equivalent to the functional spaces necessary to survive in the rental house, such as tenant rooms, toilets, kitchens, and, in building floor plans, it is equal to a graphical node. When we translate it into the WFC system, they are called SLOTS.

Boundaries of Life .

Research sites:

Hospital:
Chongqing Cancer Hospital
Chongqing Daping Hospital

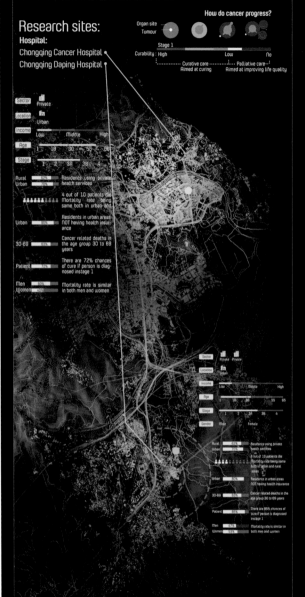

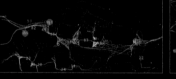

How do cancer progress?

Organ site
Tumour

Stage 1

Curability : High   Low   No

Curative care ......   Palliative care-
Aimed at curing   Aimed at improving life quality

★ In 2021, because of a community volunteer experience with an anti-cancer kitchen, I began to pay attention to the issue of medical migration in China's urbanization process. They are a neglected group in the daily public view of urbanized society mostly coming from the rural family in China. Moreover, in order to save on high hospital costs for cancer treatment, they had to live like an ant colony in high-density residential buildings with a radius of 500 meters in major cancer hospitals. These survival behaviors gave birth to the spontaneous formation of survival fissures within the building by cancer patients, their families and comfortable self-residents, and when we cut through the icy walls of these rental houses in the city, we can see the totally different life scripts of the two families.

Those real and cruel facts gave me a new understanding of the architecture profession. To my eye, the space entity between the kitchen and cancer hotel witnessed the human world. I began to reflect, as a future architect, how can I cope with those tricky situations, including future growth of the number of such households, as well as the youth and globalization of cancer incidence? How could I help them to find their own refuge in the city ?

Tracking research

By following cancer patients and their families, a whereabouts analysis is compiled to understand specifically the immediate needs of this group of people in order to better design for them.

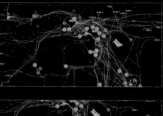

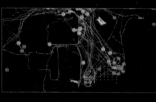

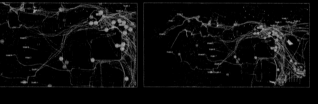

In tracking the target people, four main factors were found to be relevant to the project: the patient, the patient's family, the owner of the shared kitchen, and the furniture that had been modified.

● Patient ● Patient's family ● Owner ● Furniture

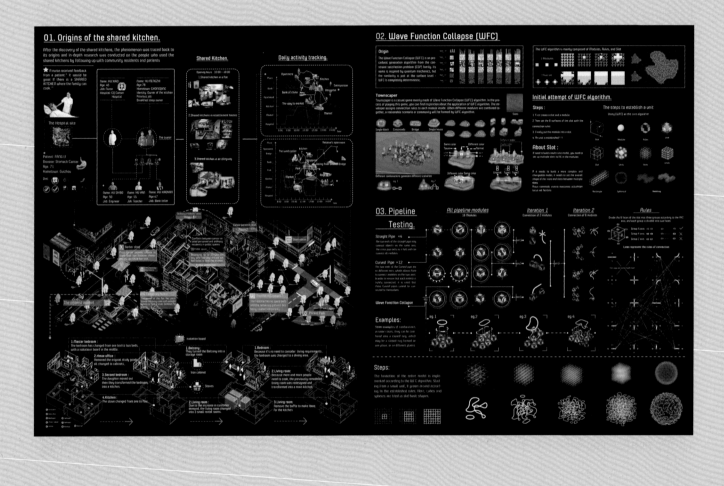

01. Origins of the shared kitchen.

After the discovery of the shared kitchens, the phenomenon was traced back to its origins and in-depth research was conducted on the people who used the shared kitchens by following up with community residents and patients.

Shared Kitchen.

Daily activity tracking.

02. Wave Function Collapse (WFC)

Origin

Townscaper

Initial attempt of WFC algorithm.

About Slot :

03. Pipeline Testing.

Straight Pipe ×4

Curved Pipe ×12

Wave Function Collapse

Examples:

Steps:

All pipeline modules

Iteration 1

Iteration 2

Rules

04. WFC indoor rules.

Try the WFC algorithm in the indoor layout, using different furnitures to test in an apartment. But in the course of use, it was found that if the rules and basic algorithms of the test pipeline are used, some unreasonable situations will appear on the furnitures.

Rules

The same combination is presented differently in different spaces. If it is in the bedroom, it will appear as a wardrobe. If it is in the clinic, it will appear as a medicine cabinet.

Connections

Modules

05. Spatial Growth Steps.

Take one floor of the building as an example for analysis, and treat the gaps and corridors between the apartments as slots, and then set the connection rules for each unit to allow these units to grow and combine in the slot. Think of these units as a compensatory space to meet the needs of residents. For example, there will be some extra small kitchens or some storage cabinets and dining tables for people to use next to the apartment that has been transformed into a shared kitchen. This is the compensation to the residents. In the beginning, only corridors connected the apartment. Gradually, small Spaces will be added in the corridor to meet the needs of residents.

Types

The original residents transformed their houses into some functions for hospital patients and caregivers, such as small hotels, physiotherapy clinics, laundry shops, shared kitchens, etc.

Space Syntax

Compensatory space syntax, which regards these small spaces grouping around the apartment as compensatory space. When these spaces appear, they can make the space syntax more perfect.

Compensatory space syntax

When various use spaces are formed in the gap between apartment 1 and apartment 2, the space syntax will be gradually improved.

06. WFC in the flat gap.

Partial details
Models under different rules.

Slots
The gaps between each apartment type on each floor are regarded as a large set of slots, in which furniture and space can be placed in the gaps according to the set rules, so that the gaps in these floors become more reasonable and efficient.

Modules
Think of a functional space as a module, and set rules for each of them before putting them into slots. Empty modules are used to form corridors between functional areas.

Rules
A line is used to express the rules between modules, and each line segment indicates that modules at the end of that line segment can be connected to each other.

Type1
Since most in this part have a large demand for storage rooms, the rules are mainly set according to storage rooms, so the number of storage rooms will be more.

Type2
Since most of the apartments in this section were converted into medical areas, there will be more medical space for them to use in the gap.

07. Rendering.

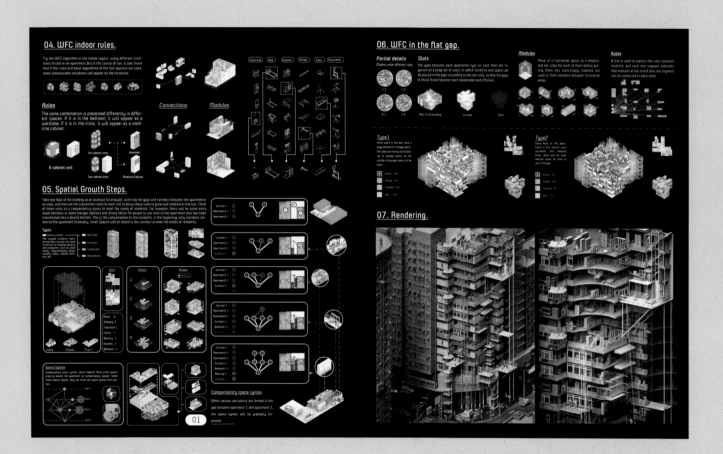

JONATHAN ARNABOLDI

MILAN, ITALY

This manifesto is inspired by the rejection of the spatial model of cities as it is now. Cities are spaces in which comfort and aberration are designed for only one of all living organisms: the human. We refuse to follow this delirious tendency, interrupting our tendency to create spaces for human entertainment and wellbeing to the detriment of other living organisms, which we call the Autochthon. A turning point is needed. The Jurban approach, elevates the Autochthon's presence despite the human. The Autochthon is considered as one big clan constituted by different tribes, each mutually contributing to the prosperity of the whole. Considering these mutual relationships, exiled humans must adapt to the Autochthon rules, and not vice versa.

The case area, fragmented and neglected by the human, will change its layout and its design; the road infrastructure will be taken over, rewilded, by Autochthon activities. Design will follow natural forces and protect the site from any human disturbance, turning into a landscape where plants and animals will live at peace. The impervious borders will ensure human absence; the articulation of the internal habitats will improve biodiversity and mutual cycles between the tribes, each of them with a role – smashing, cleaning, recycling. The road infrastructure will decline and degrade over time at the will of the tribes and, by them, will be buried. These rules embody the dynamics of a living archipelago, taking advantage from contingent disadvantages, operating an infrastructural collapse by natural dynamic cycle. In this way, breaking the rules and materiality of human presence is not just an ideological expression but a physical one as well. The Jurban Archipelago will give the benefit of a more natural course and the incipit of a disruption with the city, creating a wild habitat developing over time.

JURBAN
ARCHIPELAGO
designing for nature, not for humans

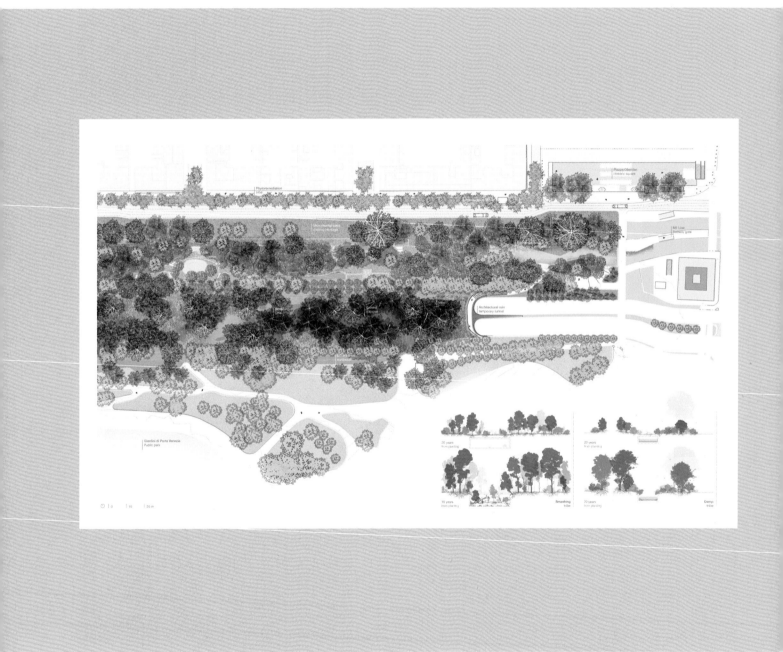

The model and the section are representative of the site's configuration after 70 years, once the tribes contributes to the degradation of human's infrastructure; the interruption with human controlled environment have as outcome a chaotic landscape in which wildness find its ease.

OLIVIA PINNER
ADAM SCOTT

>>>>>>>> MULTIPLE SITES — UNITED STATES

Decarbon-Fuzzification is an interruption that curates the decommissioning of oil refineries as a popular phenomenon. Fuzzification makes the transmutation of these deeply scarred sites soft-to-the-touch, legible, and engaging. These troubled, reckless, and harmful geographies finally receive ameliorative care that is simultaneously local support and global spectacle. All 129 United States refineries are physically draped with a massive, fuzzy, pink polyester-fleece blanket as they are decommissioned and repurposed, thereby monumentally and dynamically choreographing both a landscape and cultural transition.

Fuzzification takes immediate action in addressing some of the world's most problematic, and complex sites. Refineries are the nexus of the oil system; the system at its most legible, (quasi) public, and immediately harmful. These sites embody vehemently toxic traits and outputs that correspond with a culture dominated by the toxic masculine tendencies towards domination, control, greed, and destruction. The interruption brings attention to the fraught nature of these banal and tragically sublime geographies and establishes a hub for citizens to grapple with these sites and the toxic culture that enabled them – past, present, and future.

Fuzzification is an act of geographic introspection. A therapeutic work that highlights repair, physically and culturally, of the scars inflicted by years of extraction. These massive, air-lifted, union-made blankets embody femininity and apply fuzzy pressure to broader culture by visibly supporting, caring for, softening, and nurturing these decaying sites. Collective investment in the future of society is fostered by the catalytic spectacle of fuzzification.

LILLIAN CHUNG KWAN YU WONG OI LING ELLENA ZICHENG KAI ZHAO

LAS VEGAS, UNITED STATES

To grow up, a city must root down. Imagining the city as a tree, while it thrives for economic growth, it needs nutrients and resources. Infrastructure construction and resource extraction has always been a top-down controlled operation. Cities have been conventionally growing skyward and determined by the market. What if a city's roots can also grow organically and spontaneously downward to form the city's operational backbone?

Root city emerges as Las Vegas faces water scarcity, urban sprawl, and wealth disparity. Located beneath the gambler's city, root city is superimposed onto the existing water lines underneath the Las Vegas Strip as a way to interrupt both the capitalist system and physical configuration of a future city. It calls for bottom-up autonomy, co-ownership and co-development.

Since 2000, Las Vegas' main source of drinking water–Lake Mead–has dropped more than 150 feet in water level. Meanwhile, the surge in Vegas' homeless population has skyrocketed due to extreme capitalism, giving rise to a new community that seeks refuge in the forgotten system of underground tunnels – mole people. Inspired by this, root city describes a dystopian future scenario in 2120 with a looming water crisis and rampant homelessness. When money cannot buy water, the capital accumulated by the rich is useless. The city therefore decides to initiate an underground water diversion project and the mole people of Las Vegas become the opportunistic labor for this project.

Mole people and the government would collaborate to expand the underground infrastructure network. The empowerment of the mole people during construction of the infrastructure also induces a makeshift self-evolved autonomous underground settlement. Gradually, the once marginalized population becomes the major force operating the most important source of life – water for the upper city, accelerating their social bargaining power. The upper city and the underground city are manifested as symbiosis. The upper city depends upon nutrients from the underground for survival; the underground also needs resources from the upper city. A dynamic counterweight is thus formed to capitalism.

PIPE 201

WATER TO UPPER LAS VEGAS

PIPE 101

PIPE 104

ROOT CITY
"To grow up, a city must root down."

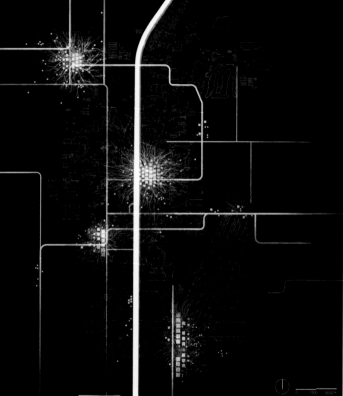

The Vegas Times

"All the News That's Fit to Print"

VOL. CXLVII . . . No. 50,967

LAS VEGAS, SUNDAY, JULY 27, 2025

60 CENTS

Late Edition
Las Vegas: Today, sunny. High 110 F. Winds SSW at 15 to 25 mph. Tomorrow, a mainly sunny sky. High 99 F. Winds S at 10 to 30 mph. Yesterday, mostly sunny skies. High near 105 F. Winds SSW at 5 to 10 mph.

VEGAS INITIATING ITS GRAND VISION OF ROOT CITY

The project offers residences and jobs for homeless, and is expected to relieve water resource disparity in the city, said an official.

BY J. R BROWN

More than 42 million tourists traveled to Las Vegas in 2018 to see the shows, the entertainers, and the gambling halls that make the city one of the nation's most popular travel destinations. The Las Vegas valley is also the home of more than 2.25 million residents, easily the most densely populated region in the state of Nevada.

What the tourists and the residents do not see, however, is a unique vision for the future that is being implemented underneath the famous Las Vegas Strip. That's where the Southern Nevada Water Authority is building organic root city as a gigantic "pumping station," a $650-million, fifteen year project that plans to open in 2040.

The project is critical to ensuring the region's water supply. When it's completed, it will have the capacity to produce more than 900 million gallons of water each day from hundreds of feet below the surface. The underground city is a sophisticated, complex, and expensive safety net that addresses the consequences of climate change. A drought that started in 2002 has caused elevation in Lake Mead to fall more than 130 feet.

"It will take more years of incredible snowpack for Lake Mead, Lake Powell, and other reservoirs to recover from this long-standing drought and the consequences of climate change," said Erika Moronis, SNWA project manager.

The Innbar pumps consist of multistage centrifugal pumps directly coupled to a submersible

electric motor in an inverted configuration and are designed for permanent submersible operation of clean water. The pumps are set with 13,000-volt motors that range from 3,150 HP to 5,200 HP. "It's really an unsung project, but it's important for the Las Vegas community to guarantee their water supply," said Tyler Ankin, project engineer for Innard.

Due to the public-private partnership nature of the project, government aims to offer jobs opportunities and residences for

increasing homeless population in the city. The enrollment details will be announced later in September.

"This will be a win-win situation for multiple shareholders: the city, residents and homeless people. It help addresses our water crisis and worsen by diasaste change, as well as an alternative way for re-engaging sinificant marginalized population in our society," said by an official during the construction inauguration.

Pipeline construction work has been inaugurated last Thursday, indicating a milestone in the city's development of Las Vegas.

There's Actually A Whole Civilization Of 'Mole People' Living Beneath Las Vegas

BY BRITTANY HAMBLETON

You likely know Las Vegas for its glittering lights, swanky casinos and million dollar hotels. What you may not know is that underneath the famed streets of the Las Vegas strip there is a whole other world. In an extensive network of tunnels running beneath the city, there lives the mole people.

This underground community is the antithesis of the city above it. Where the bright lights of the casino make it seem as though it's always daytime, in the tunnels it's always dark. While Las Vegas attracts millions of tourists of all ages every year, the underground community is one of the most dangerous places in the city.

In the autumn of 1975, a summer monsoon caused a flash flood in the Las Vegas Valley that caused millions of dollars in damage. To prevent the same thing happening again, the state began building an extensive network of tunnels beneath the city. In the case of a sudden deluge, the tunnels would redirect water underground.

There are now more than two hundred miles of tunnels that run beneath Sin City, which have become home to hundreds of the state's homeless people. These are the Mole People of Las Vegas.

The tunnels of Las Vegas rose to fame in 2002 when a man named Timmy Weber used them to hide from the authorities after he murdered his girlfriend. While the Mole People of Las Vegas do have their fair share of troubles, they are not all murderers. In fact, most of them are American citizens who, for one reason or another, have become homeless.

Sadly, many of the people who live in these tunnels struggle with addictions, substance abuse, and mental health problems. Some experts estimate that approximately three hundred people live here. The conditions in these tunnels can be challenging, and often dangerous. Matthew O'Brien, author of "Beneath the Neon: Life and Death in the Tunnels of Las Vegas," has spent countless hours down in the tunnels.

"We want to get out of here, that's always our main goal. We don't want to live like this forever," he said. "We don't like living in the tunnels.
We live here because we can, and we're not bothered by anyone.
You know, it's a lot of out-of-sight, out-of-mind."

Las Vegas has one of the worst rates of urban homelessness in the entire United States. There are approximately 5 500 homeless people in the city, but only two thousand shelter beds available.

In November 2019, the city of Las Vegas made it illegal to camp or sleep on city streets when there are shelter beds available. Violators will either receive a fine of one thousand dollars or face six months in jail.

Despite the dangers, many of the mole people do not see themselves leaving the tunnels anytime soon. Not, at least, until the city can address some of its housing problems. Until then, the dangers of living in an unpredicted, dark, and hazardous underground world are preferable to whatever waits for them above.

Sources:

Ference, Thomas. "New Project Keeps Water Running To Las Vegas." Water Online, accessed June 29, 2022. https://www.wateronline.com/doc/new-project-keeps-las-vegas-running-to-las-vegas-0001

Farfour, Joshua. "Working: The toss of strength: Southwest heat-wave health fears." The Washington Post, June 17, 2022. https://www.washingtonpost.com/climate-environment/2022/06/17/extreme-heat-las-vegas/

Jones, Judson. "A dangerous and deadly heat wave is on the way for weather stations worry." CNN June 11, 2022. https://www.cnn.com/2022/06/09/weather/heat-forecast-southwest-wednesday/index.html

The Associated Press. "Phoenix, Vegas, Denver post record temps amid Southwest heat wave. June 11, 2022. https://www.nbcnews.com/news/us-news/phoenix-denver-post-record-temps-southwest-heat-wave-rcna22191

Hambleton, Brittany. "There's Actually A Whole Civilization Of 'Mole People' Living Beneath Las Vegas." The Premier Daily, April 7, 2021. https://thepremierdaily.com/mole-people-las-vegas/

Pines, Brandon. "Together we can make a difference in our community." Las Vegas Sun, June 28, 2022. https://lasvegassun.com/news/2022/jun/28/together-we-we-can-make-a-difference-in-our-communi/

Record-breaking weekend temperatures part of Southwest heat wave

BY DAVID N. JONES

Phoenix, Las Vegas, Denver and California's Death Valley all posted record temperatures on Saturday, as dangerous heat swept across the American Southwest.

The National Weather Service in Phoenix reported a temperature of 114 degrees Fahrenheit (46 degrees Celsius), tying the record high for the date set back in 1918.

Las Vegas tied a record for the day set in 1956, with temperatures soaring to 109 F (43 C). The National Weather Service said there was a chance the high temperature in both cities could rise even more. "The first heatwave of the year has numerous climate sites threatening daily record highs and record warm lows," added the Las Vegas National Weather Service.

In Colorado, Denver hit 100 F (38 C), trying a record set in 2013 for the high temperature and the earliest

calendar ay to reach 100 F.

Temperatures in several inland areas of California have reached triple digits by the the afternoon, with a record high for June 11 of 112 F (50 C) reached in Death Valley.

Excessive heat warnings and heat advisories were issued for parts of Northern California through the Central Valley and down to the southeastern deserts.

High pressure will create a heat dome over the Western US. The dome will trap any escaping radiation and send it back to the ground, while the sun's rays continue to penetrate through.

This, combined with arid soils from an extensive and long-term drought, will allow temperatures to rise to record levels over parts of California and the Southwest, with high temperatures from the upper 90s to over 110 degrees on Friday, the Weather Prediction Center said.

'I'm not a bad person,' homelessness on the Strip has tourists fearful

BY ANNA BROWN

Times have been tough for some people and it shows around the valley. Even along the Las Vegas Strip, where the homeless have become more prevalent. As one of the most popular streets in the world, Las Vegas Boulevard offers an opportunity the some homeless to eke out a living.

"Not everyone wants to be homeless out here," said Chandler King, a musician who spends much of his time on the Strip. "I'm not a bad person, I'm an honest person, I'm a hardworking person and I just want to be treated as such, that's all."

King moved to Las Vegas from Kentucky with his girlfriend, but when the relationship came to an end, he found himself with nowhere to live.

Some tourists, however, can feel uncomfortable with the large homeless presence on the Strip.

But, Steven Campbell, a social media influencer said "the homeless are people like anyone else. A lot of them have severe problems that we don't know about."

In response to the issue of homelessness in Las Vegas, LVMPD has created the Homeless Outreach Team, with the goal to address the problem and

bring resources to those in need.

A TALE OF TWO CITIES
"Symbiosis of Above & Underground"

JIAQI LI
LEYI CUI

BEIJING, CHINA

Three hundred years of industrial civilization has largely been characterized by the human conquest of nature. A series of recent global ecological crises have called the approach of industrial civilization into question. As a result, ecological civilization was born with the primary purpose of respecting and maintaining the ecological environment.

Our proposal's site is the Shougang Factory in Beijing, China. It is one of the largest heavy industry bases in northern China, with numerous industrial buildings and equipment. This is not its first "interruption." As early as the early 20th century, the intervention of industry turned the original agricultural society in the area into an industrial civilization. The Shougang Factory helped to make human commodities abundant and the economy in the region developed rapidly. But at the same time, the consumption of the earth's resources and the damage to the environment have also accelerated sharply. Therefore, we seek to intervene here again in order to address the damage wreaked by industrial civilization by restoring the vitality of nature and making our living environment more pleasant.

Our design renovates the original Shougang Factory building, turning the former steel production site to a site of plant cultivation. We introduce biotechnology to screen and select seeds and artificial intelligence to monitor the growth of seedlings. The former factory is taken over by "nature." Such plant cultivation in former factory sites is gradually globalized, realizing the ecological restoration of the world after the grand "interruption" of world industrialization. In this way, we seek to change the narrative of human serving human to human serving nature.

Agricultural Civilization → Industrial Civilization → Ecological Civilization

Serve Human :
For People

Serve Nature :
For Nature

1919 1938 1951 1969 1979 2005 2010 2022 Tomorrow...

Plant-producing factories sprang from several major "machines"/

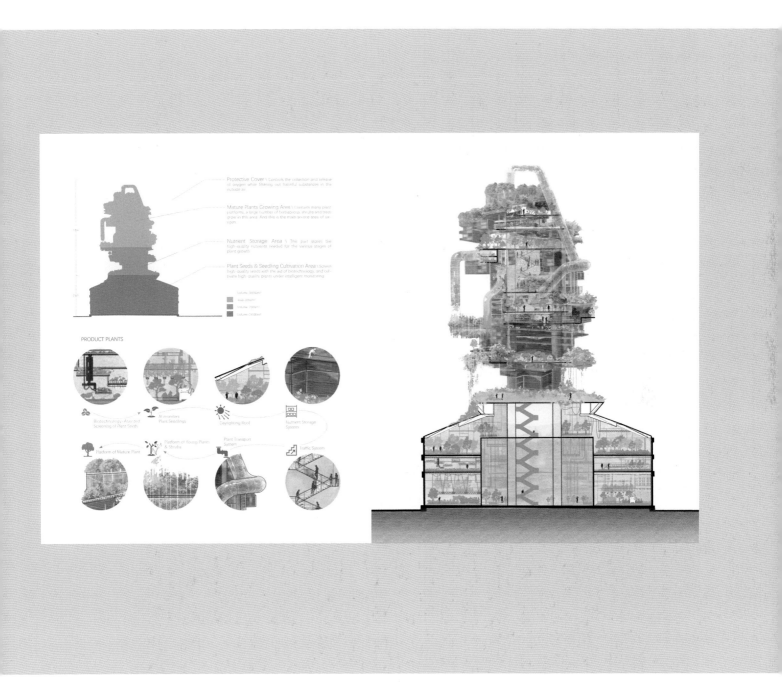

Protective Cover \ Controls the collection and release of oxygen while filtering out harmful substances in the outside air.

Mature Plants Growing Area \ Contains many plant platforms, a large number of herbaceous, shrubs and trees grow in this area. And this is the main source area of oxygen.

Nutrient Storage Area \ This part stores the high-quality nutrients needed for the various stages of plant growth.

Plant Seeds & Seedling Cultivation Area \ Screen high-quality seeds with the aid of biotechnology, and cultivate high-quality plants under intelligent monitoring.

PRODUCT PLANTS

Biotechnology-Assisted Screening of Plant Seeds

AI Intelligent Plant Seedlings

Daylighting Roof

Nutrient Storage System

Platform of Young Plants & Shrubs

Plant Transport System

Traffic System

Platform of Mature Plant

XIAOJUN ZHANG
PETER W. FERRETTO

>>>>>>>>> **GUANGZHOU, CHINA**

An agrarian village on a harbor island at the mouth of Pearl River in Guangzhou, China, is dying. Most residents have moved away, but a few continue to maintain their lives there in the face of the brutal plans for urban development of their island. At the entry of the village, a derelict market structure is left abandoned. Wandering inside the village, elements of former, more prosperous times dot the landscape, random and decaying.

We see and hear of plenty of inspiring cases of revitalization of such derelict spaces, but sometimes you just have to interrupt the instinct for survival and accept death. The farmland will soon be gone. Those we spoke to are treasuring their last dance on the soil. Before it is too late, let's build a cemetery to honor them in the market fair, trading space for memory trace. The melody of pastoral harmony is writing its last chapter, and the photographs and carved text on the tombstone shall exhibit the final lyrics. Here it comes, the elegy of the rural lands.

The Market

Harbour Island Village
1942–2022
22° 50' 37" N, 113° 31' 40" E

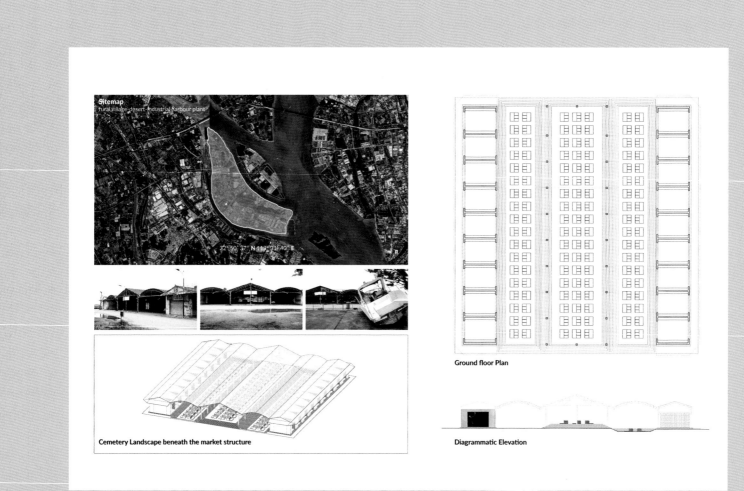

Sitemap
rural village-desert-industrial-harbour plant

22° 50' 37" N 113° 31' 40" E

Cemetery Landscape beneath the market structure

Ground floor Plan

Diagrammatic Elevation

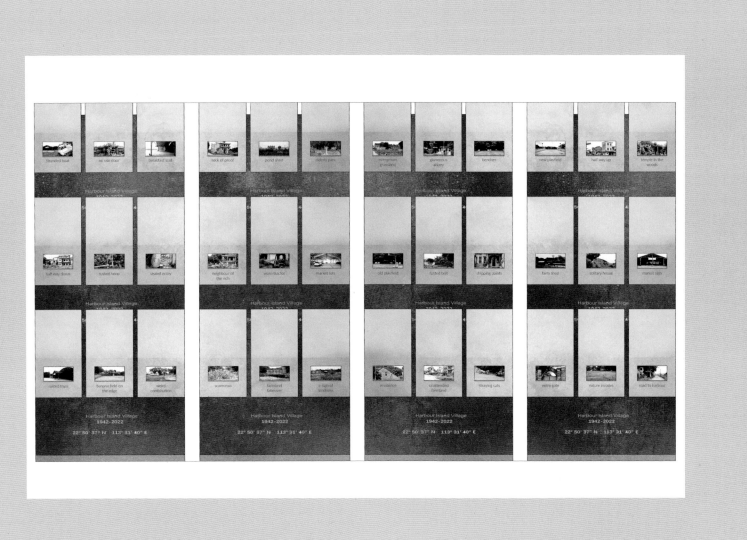

EUGENE ONG

>>>>>>>>>> BEIRUT, LEBANON

Coping, catharsis, the collective consciousness of the city. What defines adequacy when it comes to the justice of remembrance? Typically, the evidence of past traumatic events is cleared away and a pristine monument symbolizing the prior chaos is erected in its place. While it is beneficial to sometimes erase the scars of trauma for reconciliation and healing, perhaps in Beirut the trauma must be reinforced: the violence wrought upon the city and its populace kept as tactile evidence – an impactful reminder of the need for governmental vigilance and accountability.

This memorial is proposed not merely for the rebuilding of the city's fabric, but as an attempt to reexamine trust and transparency between the government and the people. In keeping–and even more drastically, occupying–the void as a new parliamentary space, the solemn duty of Lebanon's representative assembly is transferred from the halls of the historic Beirut Parliament Building into the depths of the devastation. Embedding itself into the crater and concretizing the outlines, the memorial takes on a new role as a civic site, allowing people not just to gather, grieve, and remember, but to hold accountable the decisions of the government that will henceforth be held within.

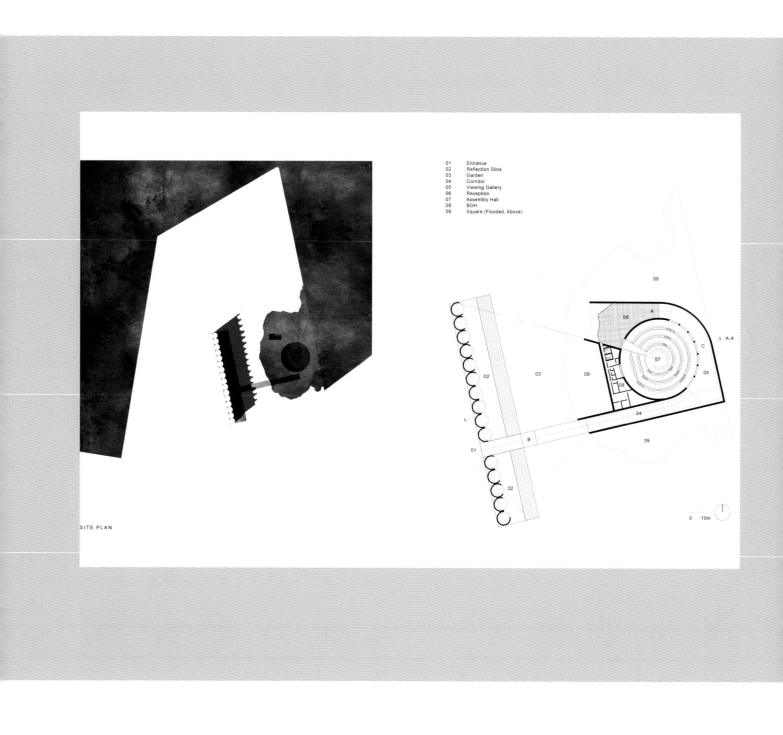

01   Entrance
02   Reflection Silos
03   Garden
04   Corridor
05   Viewing Gallery
06   Reception
07   Assembly Hall
08   BOH
09   Square (Flooded, Above)

SITE PLAN

0   10m

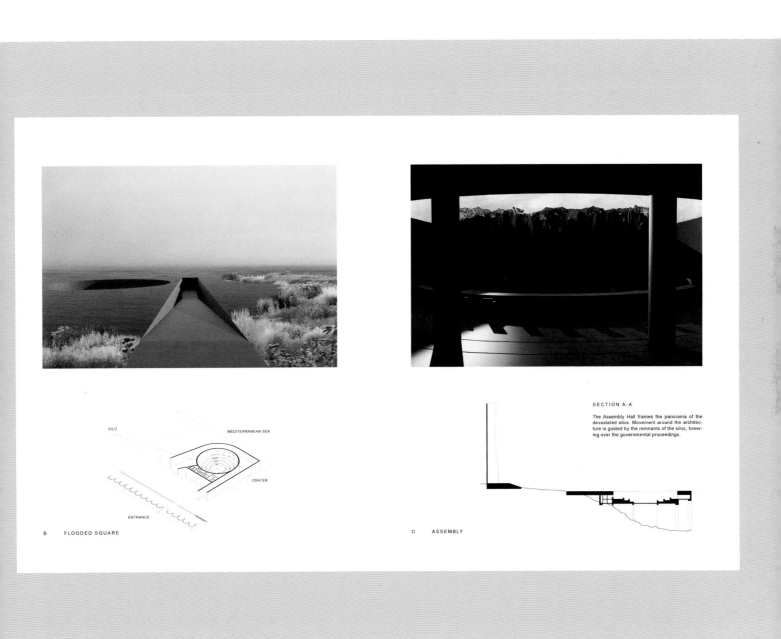

SILO
MEDITERRANEAN SEA

CRATER

ENTRANCE

B   FLOODED SQUARE

SECTION A-A

The Assembly Hall frames the panorama of the devastated silos. Movement around the architecture is guided by the remnants of the silos, towering over the governmental proceedings.

C   ASSEMBLY

YANG DU
SCOTT AKER

>>>>>>> VIRGINIA, UNITED STATES

Over recent years, critical race theory research has uncovered the depth of the slave-owning practices of some of the United States' founding fathers. Former presidents George Washington Thomas Jefferson and James Madison were together responsible for some 1,500 enslaved African Americans. These former presidents' plantations—Monticello, Mount Vernon, and Montpelier—are now tourist attractions for millions of Americans yearly. However, the slave houses, recently reconstructed, are hidden from view and an "optional" experience for tourists. We also acknowledge that the founding fathers occupied stolen land from indigenous tribes such as the Conoy, Doeg, and Monacans. These sites of trauma are essential to American history. Disruption of these patriotic tourist experiences is a top priority, including the acknowledgment of slavery and the hidden slave landscape, which is no longer a backdrop but the main storyline of these reconfigured tourist destinations.

Policy is slow by design, but reorienting landscapes can happen quickly. We want to challenge the "hero" narrative by shifting the axis of the three plantation mansions—all built by slave labor—and correct the racist "Master" site planning principles deployed by Jefferson, Washington, and Madison. This new proposal combines the three Virginia-based sites into one image that will change how people experience slave plantations by reframing the ground away from the carefully curated mansion lawns and centering the slave house as the primary experience. Our proposal acknowledges the slave trade waterways and honors the surrounding terrain worked by slave labor. The plantation's central axis—once a representation of the oppressor—is amended.

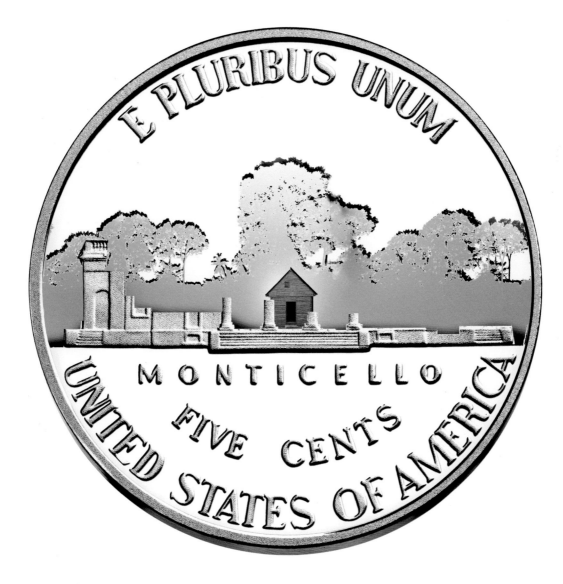

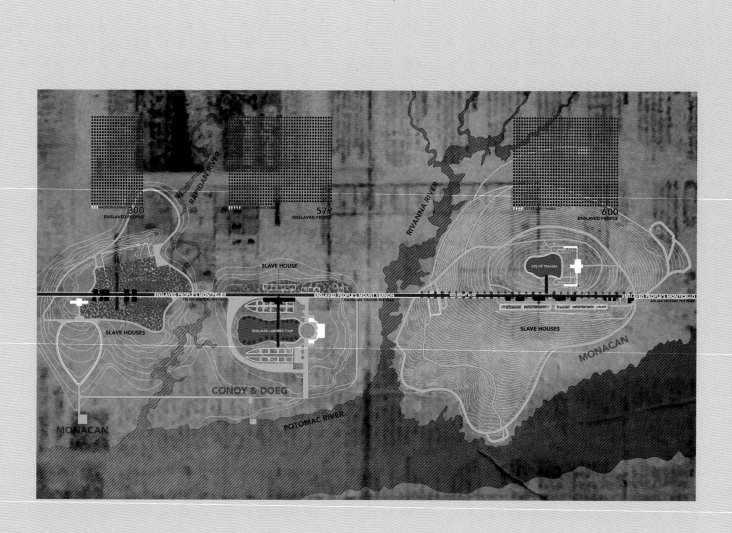

ALLEGRA ZANIRATO
REBECCA BILLI

>>>>>>> LISBON, PORTUGAL

Water, as a fluid, is conventionally associated with continuity but it often is the source of interruption with flooding in cities and the spectacle of rising seas. But are rising seas necessarily a terrible cataclysm? Is there a positive twist to be found?

Lisbon Archipelago is an attempt to answer this question by imagining a possible future for Lisbon. Due to sea level rise, the Portuguese capital is suddenly submerged by water and, for the second time after the 1755 earthquake that took down the lower area of the city, Lisbon returns to its original and most resilient configuration, with the seven oldest hills of the city left as the only inhabitable land. The hills become islands in the new Lisbon Archipelago where some landmarks emerge and some are lost to the waters creating a new perception of the city.

By its own nature, a hill is a form of interruption to the continuity of a territory. The disrupting act of flooding destroys the system of connections that define Lisbon today but introduces a new concept of uniformity. The ocean is homogeneous, it is continuous, it separates and unifies at the same time. It brings union by means of disruption.

While you may not be able to drive in this submerged Lisbon, you can swim and you can sail and explore alternative and more sustainable circulation routes and means. Tourism and the ordinary city noise have been replaced by the sound of waves, birdsong, peaceful calm, and a slower pace. Humans are not the only inhabitants, nor even the owners of the city: they now share it with fish, whales, seabirds and underwater plants. In this new landscape, while human life slows down, nature takes over. The submerged Lisbon becomes a home for all species creating a new ecology and a new way to live in the city.

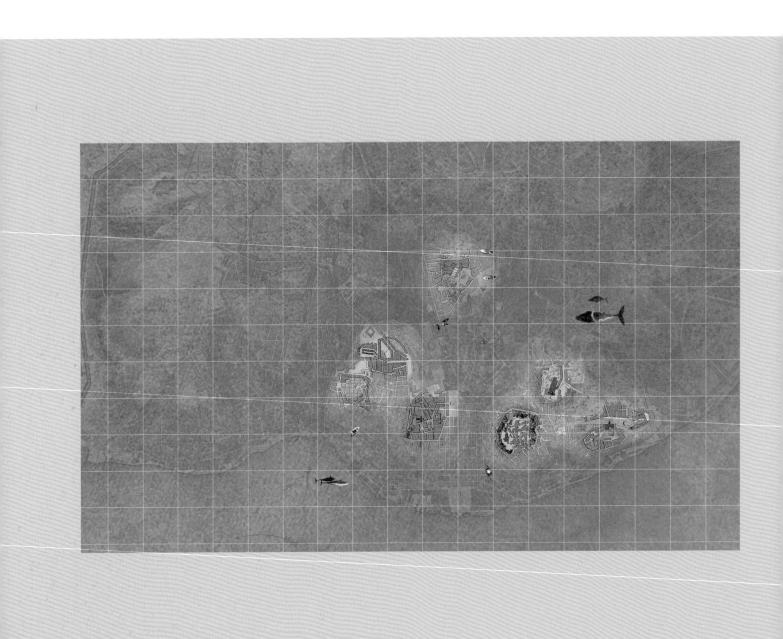

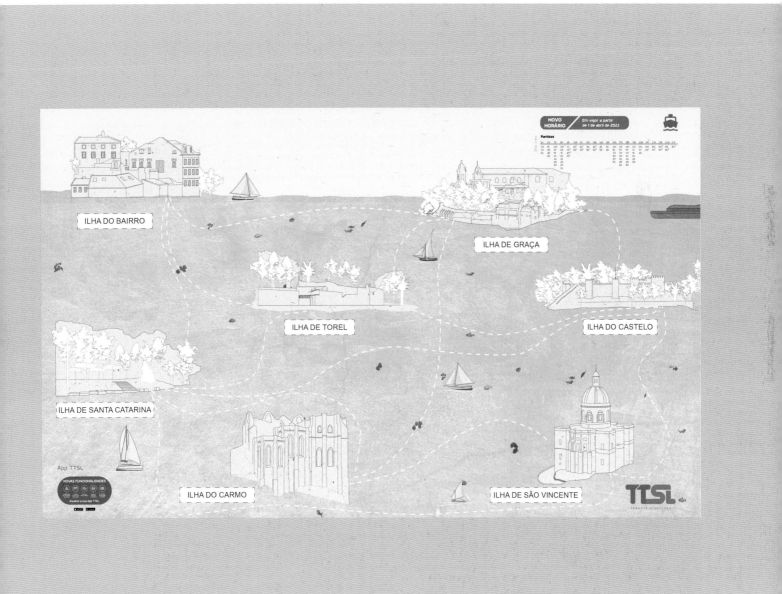

UK's housing sector is in crisis. The shortfall
ffordability and
natched anywhere. The UK's planning system
omewhat arbitrarily discriminatory in its
ply of land for new h

system is not fir for

isguide
es the shortage of land

ient, and landscape-led approach, using the

ere housing demand greatly outstrips supply, undeveloped land such as Green Belt can be phased into availability as a Growth Zone. The fundamental

ping measures to allow specific phasing and floorspace/density conditions to help developers overcome potentially high land values. Land trading and

HOME PORT - "For the Wellbeing of Everyone"

ruption 2. Dispense with standardized urban design, and let the development speak

HI THERE... ARE YOU AN ARCHITECT

ICK HAT!

SALON DES REFUSÉS

2

1. Weiran Yin: A pathway that leads people into a non-figurative interpretation of the history of the ancient town of Tucheng in Guizhou Province, China.

2. Zihao Mei: A pedestrian system designed for foot activation to reduce disease transmission through touch.

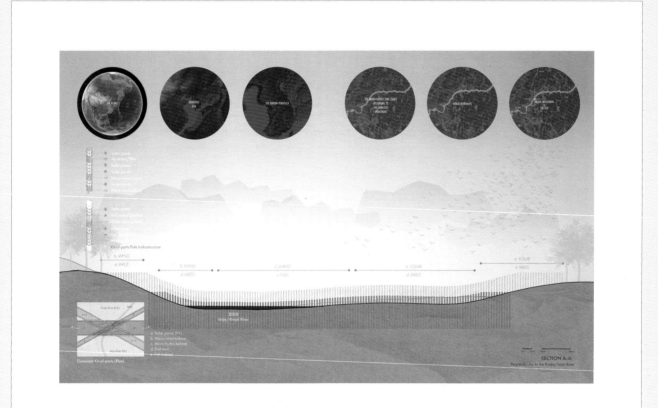

2

1. Dongsei Kim + Elise Park: A living memorial in the Demilitarized Zone between North and South Korea.

2. Tong Wu, Yuxi Xu + Ruoxi Zhang: Instead of being developed, an abandoned former military site in Milan is secured as public open space through minimal new design elements that preserve and articulate the site's history as a shooting range.

IN^{CL}_{TR}USION
— SAN SIRO —

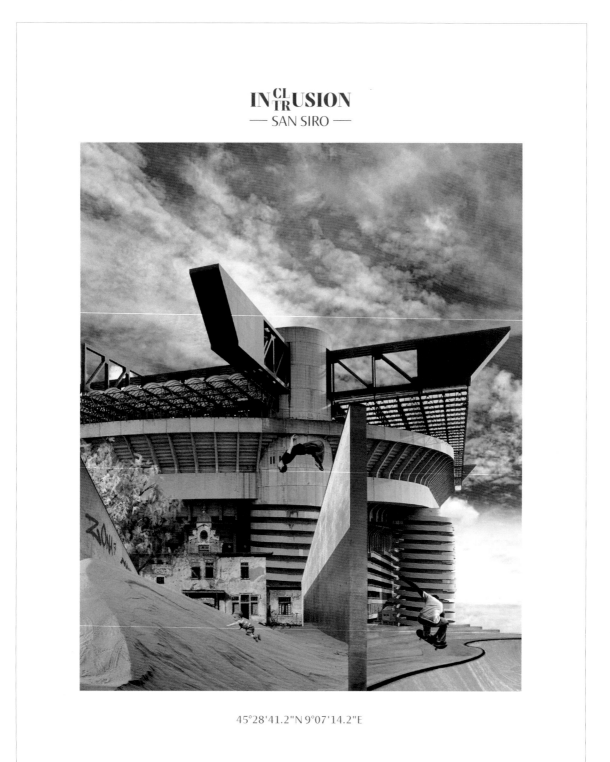

45°28'41.2"N 9°07'14.2"E

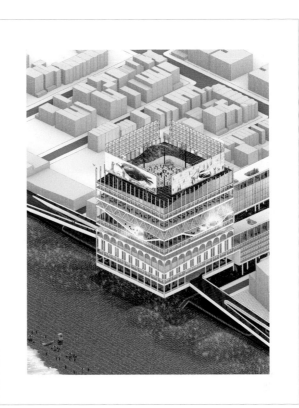

2

1. Michele Fabbro, Mirko De Roia + Francesca Fiumanò: A series of different programs are grafted onto walls cut through parts of Milan in an approach to the creation of public space that argues walls can be attractors, not dividers.

2. Matthew Scarlet: A new casino for Atlantic City that interrupts and obfuscates the city-nature border defined by the existing boardwalk, and also offers a layered stack of themed landscapes related to the city's fraught cultural history.

REVIVING THE WATERY GROUND

Activating the lost mangrove coasts of Mumbai by interrupting unplanned development on reclaimed land

Rujuta Naringrekar: Conserving and restoring Mumbai's mangroves by interrupting further urban development and landfill.

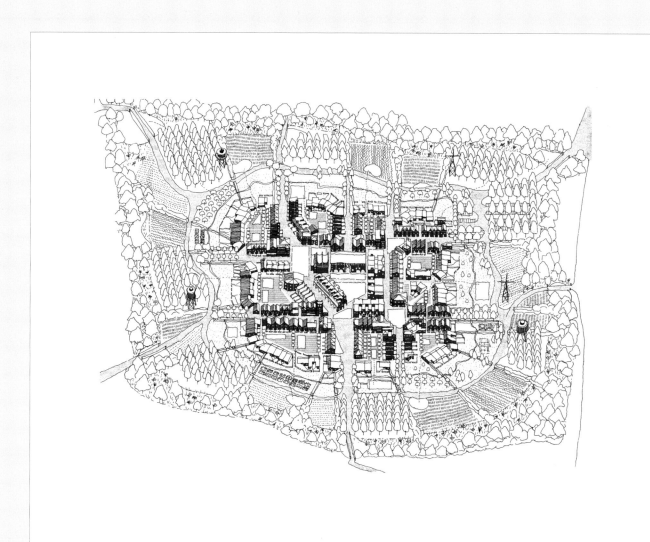

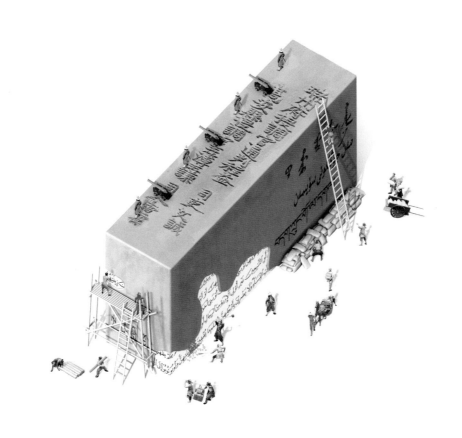

2

1. Thomas E. Ruff + Carl A. Smith: An attempt to circumvent the dualism of the English landscape and cities with scenarios for inserting affordable housing into England's National Forest.

2. Jiacheng Chen, Tian Yang + Bolei Zhang: A section of Nanjing's historic wall is interrupted with a glass insertion that aims to reveal a more nuanced history of the city in relation to its historical ethnicity.

Diego García Rodríguez + Víctor Hugo Martínez Pérez: A system of monitoring and proofing Mexico City against earthquakes.

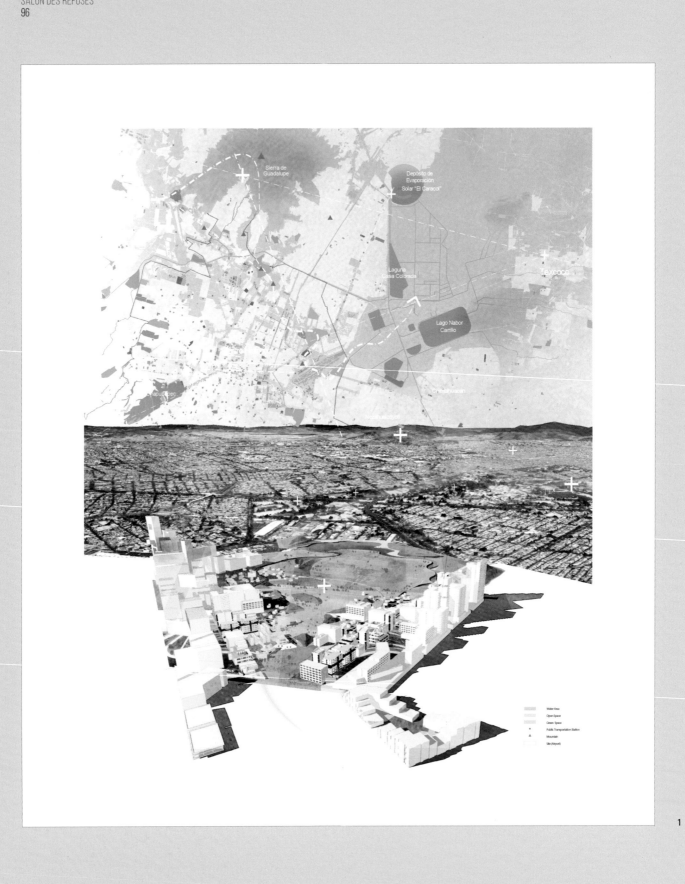

HOME PORT - *"For the Wellbeing of Everyone"*

All rights for final interpretation belong to Tangshan Office of Public Health

1. Shuya Xu, Yiwei Huang + Shreejit Modak: A form of urbanism designed to interrupt Mexico City's sprawl by creating higher density linear developments in association with open space.

2. Haoyu Wang: A system of food and health provision and green infrastructure for residential buildings experiencing long periods of COVID-related lock down in Chinese cities.

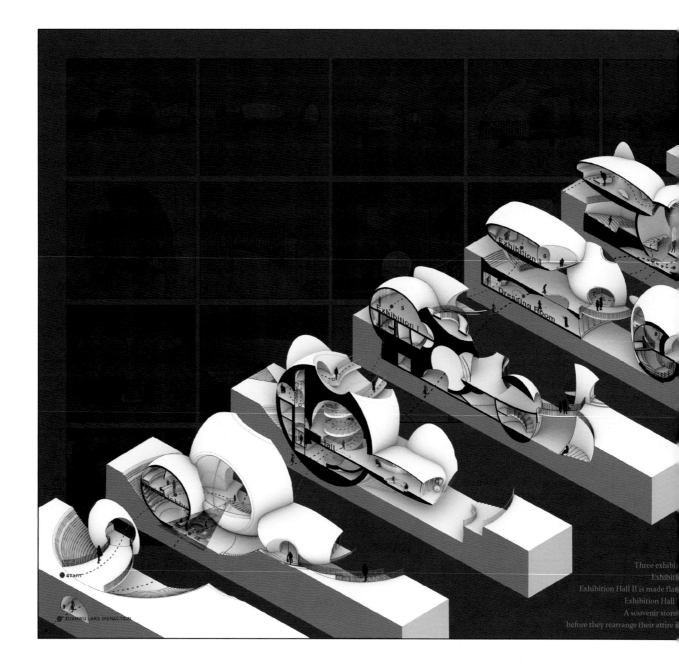

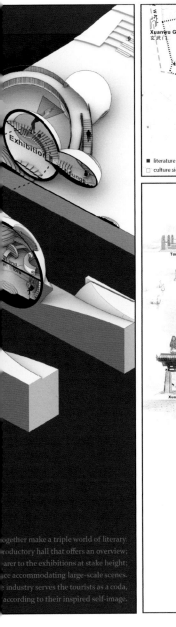

ogether make a triple world of literary
roductory hall that offers an overview;
arer to the exhibitions at stake height;
ce accommodating large-scale scenes.
e industry serves the tourists as a coda,
according to their inspired self-image.

Youyu Lu: A literary walk around Xuanwu Lake in Nanjing, China, with spaces for cultural events and exhibitions.

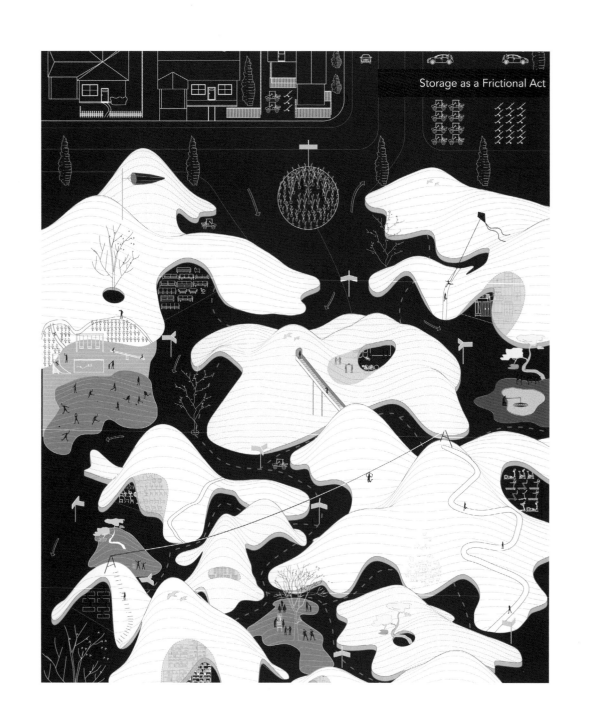

Storage as a Frictional Act

Generation Diagram

Industrial Transportation System

2

1. Wan Yan: "Storage as a frictional act" proposes to interrupt the out-of-sight, out-of-mind practice of self-storage lock-ups and create sites where objects are visible and integrated into the urban landscape.

2. Zhao Jinsong, Ren Ke + Lin Yanan: A space without perspective, rules, focus, or any meaning is proposed for a roadway cut in a mountain so that visitors can break their routines and "fill" it with their own thoughts.

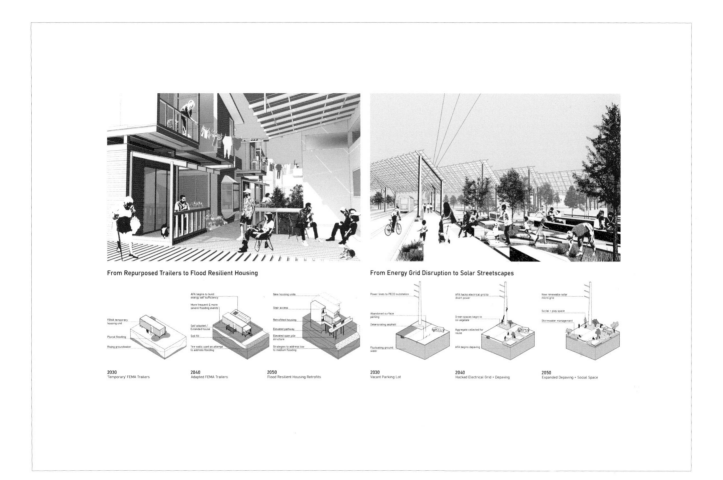

From Repurposed Trailers to Flood Resilient Housing

From Energy Grid Disruption to Solar Streetscapes

Nicole Cheng, Eduardo Martinez Villanueva + Ari Vamos:
New social spaces and housing suited to flood plains for
communities impacted by rising sea levels.

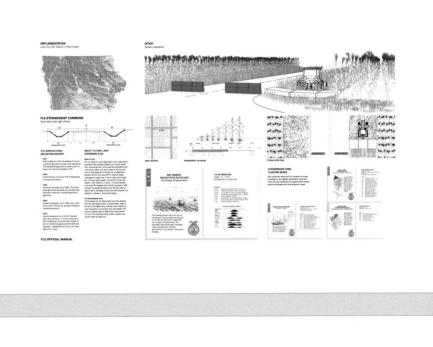

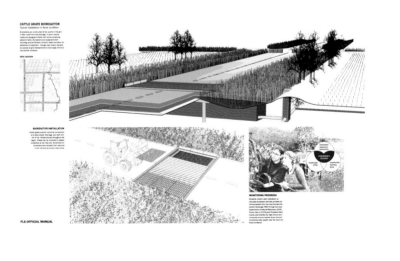

Michael J. Luegering + Anne Weber: An interruption of and addition to the Jeffersonian Grid of Iowa through reclaiming 89,420 miles of secondary road "right-of-ways" as a public commons designed as a high-performance ecosystem to help mitigate the problems of contemporary agriculture.

Ray Heikkila: A research center for students and faculty to focus on the twin themes of shelter and food outside of existing campus institutions.

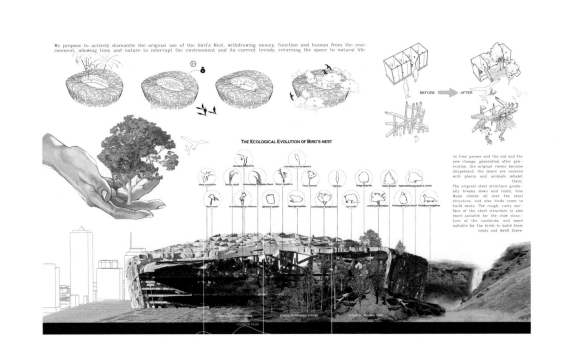

1. Zheliang Guo, Jin Zhao + Yuqian Chen: Public space related to the White Night De Flower café in Chengdu for intellectuals and poets to write whatever they want.

2. Qinxin Bai + Zihan Gao: The ruination and seeding of Herzog and De Meuron's Beijing Olympic Stadium as the centerpiece of a larger project to restore ecological vitality to Beijing.

Bede Brennan: The replacement of the grass monoculture (and its suburban and colonial symbolism) covering Australia's Parliament House with a diversity of grasses endemic to the Australian ecosystem.

Cristina Vicente-Gilabert + Carmen Armenteros-Puchades: The monuments of Rome are removed to the peri-urban outskirts of the city so as to deflect tourism from the center and raise questions about the city's future.

Steve Valev: The individual body is the first site of interruption in order to break with ubiquitous conformity known as "American Smooth."

THE HEATHERWICK HAT ™

HI THERE... ARE YOU AN **ARCHITECT?** WANT TO GO **GREEN?** HERE'S **HOW TO DO IT!**

INTRODUCING... **THE HEATHERWICK HAT!**

COMPONENTS:

| 1. INTERIOR SCAFFOLDING | 2. IRRIGATION AND CAPILLARY FEEDING TUBES | 3. GEOTEXTILE LAYER | 4. PLANTS* |

- COMPONENTS 1-3 ARE TO BE INSTALLED ON THE ARCHITECT BY A **SPECIALIST CONTRACTOR.**

- A SPECIALLY-TRAINED **HARDWICK HATWEAVER** MUST BE ENGAGED TO INTEGRATE THE PLANTS INTO THE GEOTEXTILE, UNDER SUPERVISION OF A QUALIFIED HORTICULTURALIST.

*PLANTS ARE TO BE A SPECIALLY-BRED SUBSPECIES GRAFTED ONTO ROOTSTOCK SOURCED FROM **AMAZONIAN RAINFOREST**

DURING THE ESTABLISHMENT PERIOD IT IS **VITAL** THAT THE **MAINTENANCE AND INSPECTION SCHEDULES** AND **GENERAL CARE REQUIREMENTS** ARE ADHERED TO.

- DAILY: IRRIGATION AND GENERAL INSPECTION
- WEEKLY: WEEDING
- FORTNIGHTLY: FLUSH-OUT TUBING
- MONTHLY: HORTICULTURAL INSPECTION AND FERTILISING
- SIX MONTHS: STRUCTURAL INSPECTION OF SCAFFOLDING
- ETC.
- etc.

IT IS RECOMMENDED THAT THE ARCHITECT AVOID VERY **HOT, DRY, WINDY, COASTAL AND COLD** ENVIRONMENTS.

IN FACT, IT'S PROBABLY BEST IF THE ARCHITECT DOESN'T MOVE AROUND TOO MUCH **AT ALL.**

ONCE THE ESTABLISHMENT PERIOD HAS PASSED, **THE HAT** (IF PROPERLY MAINTAINED) WILL BEGIN TO ATTRACT **INSECTS,** WHICH WILL USE IT AS A **HABITAT.**

THIS DOES NOT INDICATE IMPROPER FUNCTIONING OF **THE HAT,** HOWEVER IT MAY CAUSE **INSTABILITY** IN THE ARCHITECT.

OVER TIME, WITH THE BUILD-UP OF **VEGETATIVE MATERIAL,** SMALL **BIRDS** AND EVEN **MAMMALS** CAN BE EXPECTED TO TAKE UP RESIDENCE ON THE ARCHITECT!

ONE OPTION IS TO INSTALL A SYSTEM OF **STRUTS** AND **TENSIONED CABLES** TO PREVENT EXCESSIVE LATERAL MOVEMENT IN THE ARCHITECT.

ALTERNATIVELY, IF THE ARCHITECT IS VERY **TIRED,** THEY MAY PREFER TO FALL **IN-SITU** AND COME TO REST ON THE **GROUND PLANE.**

WHICHEVER OPTION IS SELECTED, THE ULTIMATE RESULT WILL BE THE SAME: A **BEAUTIFUL,** HIGHLY **STABLE VEGETATED MOUND** WITH AN INTEGRATED SOURCE OF **NUTRIENTS** AND AN **ESTABLISHED ECOSYSTEM.**

EDITOR'S CHOICE

Anna Feldman, Gagani Warnakulasooriya + Danyelle Bailey: A structure designed to support the growth of plants over the human body, developed as a satirical response to the insincere and ubiquitous "greening" of architecture projects. Rather than installing plants on structures, architects can simply don the Heatherwick Hat.

IN THE NEXT ISSUE OF

LA+

As designers, we strive to make, to shape, and to depict beautiful things, places, and environments. Yet while beauty is central to our praxis, it is neither objective nor universal, and defining it is not an easy task. Beauty can be appreciated visually or intellectually: it takes on different forms and has different meanings in different cultures and contexts. What, then, do we mean when we describe something as beautiful? Or, perhaps more interestingly, how do definitions of beauty designate that which is not? **LA+ BEAUTY** examines the concept of beauty as it relates to landscape architecture and the constructed environment. What is a "beautiful" landscape today? Is there such a thing as "natural beauty"? Why do humans across the cultural spectrum concern themselves so much with the beautification of themselves, their objects, and their surroundings? Is beautification benevolent or nefarious? Is there value—economic or otherwise—in beauty, and whose interests do ideals of beauty serve? In the end, why does beauty matter at all?

LA+ BEAUTY is guest-edited by Colin Curley.

ELSA ANDERSON

VINCENT BAPTIST

ADRIAN BEJAN

JEFFREY BLANKENSHIP

JACKY BOWRING

WINIFRED CURRAN

JESSICA HAYES-CONROY

GRETCHEN HENDERSON

NICHOLAS HOLM

ELIZABETH MEYER

LUKE MORGAN

MARIAGRAZIA PORTERA

MICHELLE STUHLMACHER

BRANDI THOMPSON SUMMERS

SAREM SUNDERLAND

DAN VAN DER HORST

SASKIA VERMEYLEN

LIBBY VIERA-BLAND

OUT FALL 2023

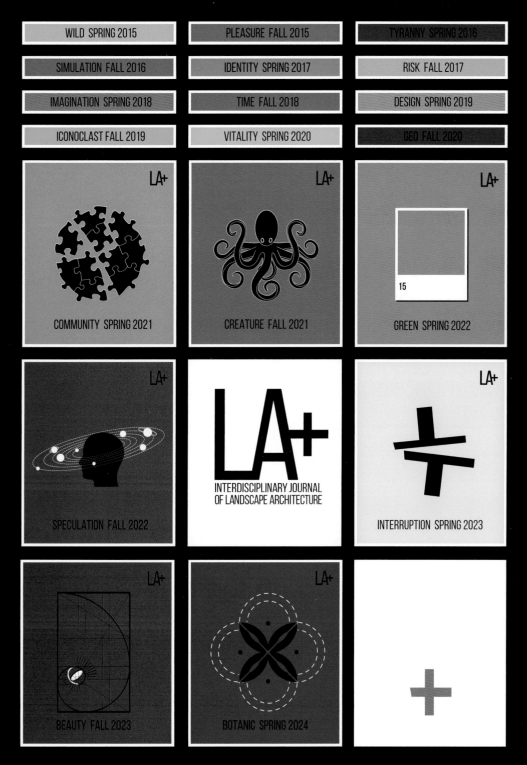

WILD SPRING 2015	PLEASURE FALL 2015	TYRANNY SPRING 2016
SIMULATION FALL 2016	IDENTITY SPRING 2017	RISK FALL 2017
IMAGINATION SPRING 2018	TIME FALL 2018	DESIGN SPRING 2019
ICONOCLAST FALL 2019	VITALITY SPRING 2020	GEO FALL 2020

COMMUNITY SPRING 2021

CREATURE FALL 2021

GREEN SPRING 2022

15

SPECULATION FALL 2022

LA+
INTERDISCIPLINARY JOURNAL
OF LANDSCAPE ARCHITECTURE

INTERRUPTION SPRING 2023

BEAUTY FALL 2023

BOTANIC SPRING 2024

LA+ (Landscape Architecture Plus) from the University of Pennsylvania Weitzman School of Design is the first truly interdisciplinary journal of landscape architecture. Within its pages you will hear not only from designers, but also from historians, artists, philosophers, psychologists, geographers, sociologists, planners, scientists, and others. Our aim is to reveal connections and build collaborations between landscape architecture and other disciplines by exploring each issue's theme from multiple perspectives.

LA+ brings you a rich collection of contemporary thinkers and designers in two issues each year. To subscribe follow the links at WWW.LAPLUSJOURNAL.COM.